Contents

Page

Foreword

This is now the fourth and fully revised edition of my helicopter manual. I wrote the first part about 10 years ago and many things have altered in the meantime. Many branches of the industry concerned with helicopters, model suppliers, control systems and accessories have grown and new knowledge has come on to the scene. Thousands have learnt to fly helicopters in the meantime and many more start daily.

One could write volumes, discuss for weeks on end and have so much to say, but the length of the book is limited and so I have decided not to mention obsolete models but to correct some opinions, add new information and concentrate on developing the photo explanations and detail descriptions. Apart from anything else the one dominating wish remains to share with the reader the basic knowledge and the fascination for flying model helicopters, to introduce him to the 'secret' of this interesting hobby and fill him with enthusiasm for this sport.

When you have read the following account of my first flight you will understand what I mean.

Greetings

Dieter Schlüter

I. Introduction

Sunday, 12.4.1970—Jüngesheim flying site, near Frankfurt am Main.

Flight Report:

'. . . and so after perhaps 5 or 6 hovering flights of about 10 minutes each, I felt I was beginning to get the measure of the helicopter. My control of it was by no means precise and secure, let alone skilful. But the model no longer had the upper hand, and I had a fair chance of setting it down where I intended.

The next stage was my first 'circuit'.

I must admit that I really did not intend it to fly away from me, but suddenly it had happened, and there was no going back. I very timidly began to ease the model into forward flight. First 5 m., then 10 m, then 15. Suddenly it was at 20—25 m, climbing far too fast, and accelerating forwards. It had reached the end of the site, where the tall grass began—what now? Less forward cyclic, increase throttle slightly, hold it on course and wait. Before I knew what was happening, the machine was 20—25 m up and about 80—100 m away from me.

What now? Turn it round!

Right then, a gentle turn, just don't crash it now! The model is banking, but doesn't turn. 150 metres away now, and 30—35 metres up. Stop, for Heaven's sake! Feed in a little tail rotor. It works! The machine is coming round, looking fine. Hold altitude, don't panic! Through 180° now, straighten up, off with the turn, correct tail rotor.

Here it comes!—I feel relief and anxiety at the same time.

Now the model is above me, far too high, 30—40 metres. And still it's climbing, higher and higher.

Let's turn her again; that's better already; the machine will put up with very large control movements, more than I would ever have believed. The model is sideways on to me now, still climbing. I must do something about that climb if I want to take the machine home in one piece. Throttle back, then more—it won't come down! On the contrary, now it's heading off forwards, slowly and elegantly, and the motor is puttering at about half throttle; you can hear the blades throbbing. How long have I been up? Two minutes, three minutes? I don't know. Good Lord, how much fuel was in the tank? No idea.

Okay then, let's land before it's too late. Throttle back even further, the model is right over the spot. Now she's sinking, gently at first, then faster, suddenly too fast! Open the throttle—last chance—the motor picks up, the model recovers. But . . . I've forgotten the tail rotor and the increased torque. The machine turns 180° left, and the nose drops. Faster and faster, diving at about 45° straight at me and my colleagues.

That's it, it's finished. Just a heap of wreckage.

But no, full throttle and pull hard back on the stick—and it works. The nose rises, the machine is flying at a fantastic speed, and thunders past us at about 2 m altitude. In an instant it is 25—30 m high again. Phew, fortune smiles on me again—and what good fortune. I would never have believed that the model could recover from such a situation.

So it works, control is good, power is adequate even for that sort of situation. The thought flashes across my mind—I will stick with this method of control.

Fig. 1: The 'Bell Huey Cobra', the world's first radio-controlled model helicopter. Taken after the first five minute circuit on 12.4.1970.

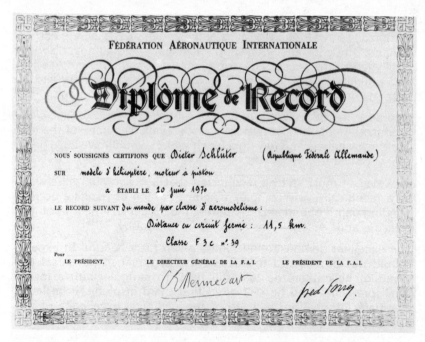

FÉDÉRATION AÉRONAUTIQUE INTERNATIONALE

Diplôme de Record

NOUS SOUSSIGNÉS CERTIFIONS QUE *Dieter Schlüter* (*République Fédérale Allemande*)

SUR *modèle d'hélicoptère, moteur à piston*

a ÉTABLI LE *20 juin 1970*

LE RECORD SUIVANT *du monde par classe d'aéromodélisme :*

Distance en circuit fermé : 11,5 km.

Classe F 3 c n° 39

Pour
LE PRÉSIDENT,

LE DIRECTEUR GÉNÉRAL DE LA F.A.I.

LE PRÉSIDENT DE LA F.A.I.

Fig. 2: The diplomas for the two world's records set on 20.6.1970.

But what now, the model is still up there! So, the same procedure again, but carefully this time. It seems like an eternity, struggling with that landing. It gets away from me twice more, just like before, but not so critically. And then—I've made it. 6—8 metres up, right over the spot, and down it comes to settle gently in front of me.

No damage, not a scratch; just as if that flight was an everyday occurrence.

A roar goes up—people are clapping, friends thump me on the shoulder, but it is no good talking to me. I am exhausted, absolutely worn out. How long was I up there, then? More than five minutes, comes the reply. I can scarcely believe it. It seemed like an eternity!'

That report of my first helicopter circuit, which lasted over five minutes and ended successfully, appeared in the July issue of 'Modell' magazine in 1970. It described the successful conclusion of a line of development which had occupied many years, involving a vast number of theories, ideas, experiments and failures. The occasional partial success spurred me on again and again to conquer the problem of the radio-controlled model helicopter.

Over the years, I acquired such a wealth of data and experience that I was gradually able to solve the numerous problems, and my technical knowledge was constantly widening. This research, in conjunction with the workshop facilities I had at my disposal, finally led to the success described above, which was crowned by two official world records on 20th June 1970 – 27 minutes and 51 seconds duration, and 11.5 km distance over a closed circuit.

And now, in 1986, a large number of (almost) perfect, commercially produced model helicopters are already available, many of them of scale appearance, and having a finish which would have been just a dream only a few years ago.

However, it must still be recognized that a helicopter will always be a technically very complex machine, which demands a corresponding depth of understanding from the modeller, if he is to obtain pleasure and personal satisfaction from his hobby.

The excellent demonstration flights given by a handful of experts should not be allowed to deceive the beginner; if he enters the world of helicopters he will still have to struggle with a lot of small problems, and he will often find them insoluble if he lacks adequate information. In spite of the technical excellence of the machines, he will probably make the occasional mistake which slips

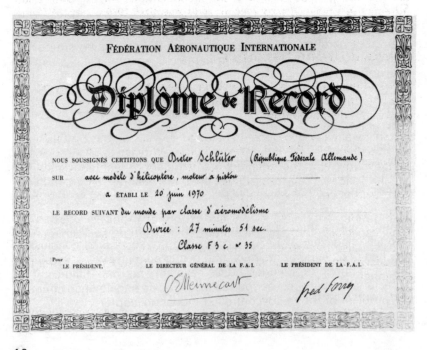

through because of his lack of experience, and which can ultimately result in disappointment.

The purpose of this book is to provide a source of basic information about the technology of helicopters in general, and of model helicopters in particular; to explain the relevant aerodynamics, and to demonstrate the most important mathematical calculations. One section of the book is devoted entirely to constructional problems, the individual components and their function, the installation of the radio system, the controls, and finishing. The problems of trimming a model, training for the beginner and the advanced flyer, and maintenance and repair, are also covered.

My description of the development of model helicopters is not intended just to give an idea of the large number of problems encountered early on, but is meant to serve the modeller as a guide when he is carrying out his own experiments. Above all it will help him to avoid failures, and to avoid repeating the mistakes which were made in the initial development period.

In the midst of all the enthusiasm, the question of safety must never be forgotten. For this reason the reader should pay particular attention to the sections concerning safety, both relating to flying and preparing these machines, so that colleagues and spectators can join in the pleasure and technical fascination of helicopter flying without any undue risk.

A word to the beginner

I am often asked what is the best way into helicopter flying for the beginner, to ensure a measure of success as quickly as possible, and avoid disappointment.

You have already taken the first step to success by buying this book and reading this far. Keep on reading! At least read these initial suggestions, and the chapters 'Constructional techniques for the model helicopter', 'Accessories', 'A day's flying', 'Flight training' and 'On the subject of safety'.

Flying radio controlled model aircraft is not exactly a cheap pastime, especially if you take it seriously and set your sights high. But you can also overdo it. It is not always necessary to buy the most expensive, and the dearest is not always the best. Especially for the beginner.

Here is my advice:
The beginner to the world of helicopters should opt initially for a system which provides a low cost introduction, with a simple,

understandable mechanical system. However, it should also be capable of extension to keep pace with the beginner's increasing skill. This applies to the mechanics, the rotor system, and the bodywork, plus accessories and detail fittings. Be careful that the model is easily serviceable, that means that all parts are easy to get to and can be repaired. Also find out whether spare parts will be easily obtainable after a while. It is also important to be able to fit varying motors, perhaps other than the one you have. This is the same for the radio control units.

Above all, don't make the mistake of trying to imitate the flying aces and their aerobatics. As beginners you have a whole load of other worries first and are a long way from the achievements of the experts.

The commonest question at this stage is—what is the best rotor system for the beginner?—It is also the hardest question to answer. It always depends on how much the 'beginner' actually knows, to what extent he will develop an understanding of the model, and whether he has to rely on his own resources, or can expect help from fellow modellers.

Let's imagine: you have an elaborate model with all the refinements, everything perfectly adjusted and the model test-flown. You have a really experienced model helicopter pilot standing next to you, perhaps with a second teacher/pupil (buddy box) transmitter. Nothing can really go wrong here. If teacher and pupil are good, or very good, then the pupil is bound to pick up rapidly the art of helicopter flying.

Whether this pupil will have learned how to tune his motor accurately, how to adjust and correct the rotor head, how to trim out his model correctly, and a hundred other little 'wrinkles', is debatable, to say the least. Everything takes time.

If you have had experience with 'normal' model aircraft, matters such as motor settings, recognizing certain flight situations and trimming out the model, will not worry you unduly. Your experience in *controlling* such models will unfortunately be virtually no help, at least in hovering flight. Nevertheless, even if you have a sophisticated, complex model, you will quickly master the flying if you have a 'teacher' by your side.

But if you really are a beginner, (infant prodigies excepted) and there is no expert assistance to hand, then you have no choice: start simply. Forget the dramatic flying of the experts; don't listen to the advice of your friends—often they know less about it than you do— and lay your dreams to one side for a while. Come back to earth—

that is where your model helicopter is. First learn to take off, to hover at 1–2 m altitude, to maintain a heading, to hover from one side to the other and back. Then, later, simple circuits. You do not need any kind of super-model for all this, just a good and solid construction with a robust rotor head. You are bound to turn your model over a few times at this stage, and there are far fewer parts to break. It is therefore much more straightforward and quick to repair and re-adjust. Nobody learns to ride a bicycle on a racing cycle with gears; you pick a simple machine which can take the inevitable knocks. If you selected the right helicopter system from the beginning – one with the widest range of accessories and conversions – you can develop your model as far as you want; right up to a fully aerobatic model capable of loops, rolls, inverted flying etc., if you wish.

But stop – enough of this. Just get started for now, and console yourself with the thought that those experts had to start where you are now. All of them – myself included.

With this thought I would like to wish you a lot of success and pleasure in our mutual hobby.

Dieter Schlüter.

II. The basics of helicopter technology

This chapter is intended to provide a summary of the essential inter-related factors involved in the flight, the drive system and the control system of the helicopter. A knowledge of these factors is valuable for the understanding of the mechanics and the problems of the model helicopter.

1. From the fixed wing aircraft to the helicopter

An orthodox fixed wing aircraft, as is well known, requires a certain forward speed in order to fly. This motion is provided by a propeller, or other source of thrust. The forward speed produces a flow of air over the lifting surfaces, which is able to keep the aircraft in the air. The stabilising tail surfaces of a fixed wing aircraft also need a certain forward speed and the resulting flow of air in order to function.

The helicopter operates on a different principle. The flying machine does not need to be given a certain forward speed; the aircraft

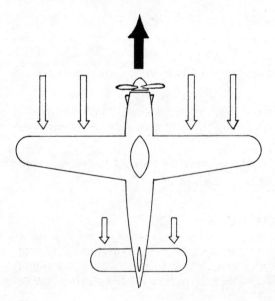

Fig. 3:
Fixed wing aircraft. The airflow over the wings is a result of the forward speed of the whole aircraft.

can be allowed to remain motionless. In contrast to the fixed wing aircraft, with its wings rigidly mounted to the fuselage, the helicopter's 'wings' are able to rotate like a large propeller. The motive power of the machine is used, not to move the whole aircraft forward, but to actively rotate the flying surfaces. Hence the term 'rotary wing aircraft'. The rapid rotation of the flying surfaces produces a flow of air over them, and their aerodynamic shape provides a lifting force which is capable of raising the helicopter. The helicopter can therefore hover over one point without moving forward.

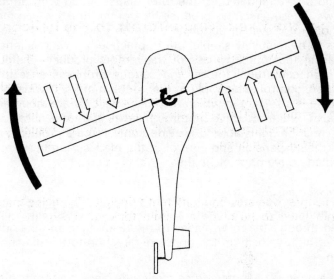

Fig. 4: Helicopter, or rotary wing aircraft. The airflow over the 'wings' (blades) is caused by the rotation of the whole rotor system. The flying machine itself need not move.

The entire rotating system, which revolves on a common axis, is called the helicopter's 'rotor', and the lifting surfaces are known as 'rotor blades'.

There are helicopters with one or more rotors, and rotors with two or more rotor blades.

2. Rotor drive systems

Various basic systems can be used to drive the rotor. The first group comprises the 'blade-drive systems', in which as the name implies, the rotors are driven directly by the blades. In the case of

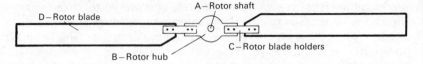

Fig. 5: The rotor, and the names of the most important components:
A = rotor shaft   C = blade holders
B = rotor hub   D = rotor blades

Propeller drive

small motors are situated on the rotor blades, fitted with orthodox airscrews. These airscrews produce horizontal thrust, which moves the whole rotor system about its common axis. The drive system appears to be relatively simple, but in practice has various inherent drawbacks; the rotating mass of the motors produces extraordinarily high centrifugal forces, and serious problems arise in the lubrication, control and supply of fuel to the motors. A variation on this theme is a system in which the airscrews only are mounted on the blades, while the drive motor is fixed to the rotor hub. As the blades must be adjustable to provide control, more problems arise here in the suspension and control of the blades. Another example of the blade drive principle is the

Compressed air drive system

Here a compressor or a turbine produces compressed air, which is pumped through the rotor blades to the blade tips, and they direct the air at high velocity in the opposite direction to the direction of rotation.

This also provides a motive force, which displaces the rotor system in the required direction. The problems in this system are centred on the design of the rotor blades, which have to be of sufficiently

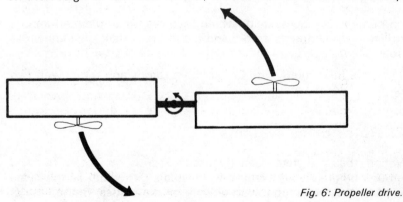

Fig. 6: Propeller drive.

large cross section to allow an adequate throughflow of air. The rotor heads are also relatively complex to make, the air-tight seals being a special problem.

Jet propulsion

is a further variant of this system. In this case the jet engines or ram jets are mounted directly on the blade tips, producing thrust at a tangent to the direction of rotation. Here again the rotor blades, and in particular the blade connections, are subject to very high loads, as a result of the enormous centrifugal forces involved. These systems also develop exceptionally high noise levels.

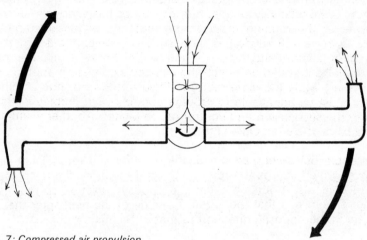

Fig. 7: Compressed air propulsion.

The major disadvantage of all blade drive systems lies in their relatively poor efficiency. This is due to the fact that the power produced by the motors cannot be used directly to drive the rotor, but has to drive the rotor via the air, which is a relatively inefficient medium. Hence a large proportion of the power developed by the motors is lost when used in a blade drive system. These systems do have appreciable advantages however, in that they eliminate geared drives, clutches, freewheels etc. Another point in their favour is that no torque is transferred to the fuselage via the drive system. This is not the case with

Shaft drive systems

Here the rotor is directly driven via the main rotor shaft. This eliminates the power-sapping effects of the blade drive system, and almost

17

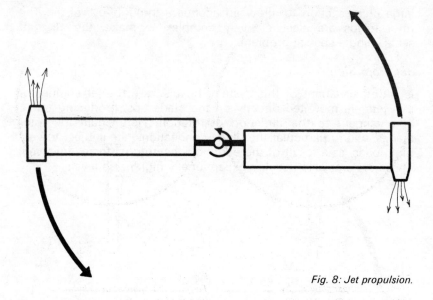

the entire power output is available to drive the rotor. That same power which causes the rotor shaft, and therefore the main rotor, to revolve, also exerts an equal and opposite reaction on the fuselage. This means that the whole fuselage of the helicopter tries to rotate in the opposite direction to that of the main rotor.

3. Torque compensation

The turning force exerted on the fuselage has to be counteracted by a special torque compensation mechanism. Here the possibilities are as follows:

Torque compensation by means of a side propeller

A normal, but variable pitch airscrew is fitted to the side of the fuselage, and is used to provide an amount of thrust which exactly counteracts the torque. The advantage of this arrangement is that it can be used to provide extra forward thrust when the helicopter's forward speed increases. The disadvantage is that the airscrew always has to be reset precisely to match each change in forward speed, and in torque, in order to stop the fuselage rotating away from the direction of flight. A further possibility is:

18

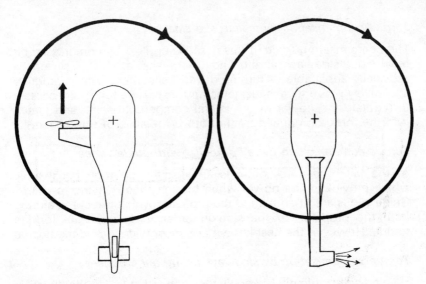

Fig. 9:
Torque compensation by means of side-mounted propeller

Fig. 10:
Torque compensation by means of side jet.

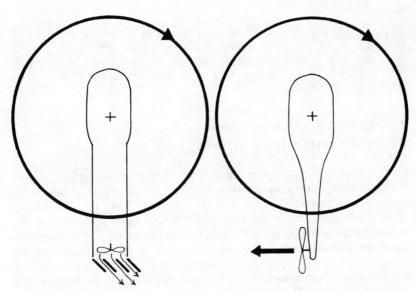

Fig. 11:
Torque compensation by means of tail propeller with adjustable vanes.

Fig. 12:
Torque compensation by means of side-mounted tail propeller (tail rotor).

19

Torque compensation by means of a side jet

The compensating force in this case is supplied by compressed air blown out sideways at the end of the fuselage. This system is especially applicable to turbine driven helicopters, which produce a relatively powerful exhaust jet in any case. Here too it is necessary to regulate the power of the lateral compensation jet, and match it to the torque produced by the rotor. A relative of this system is:

Torque compensation by tail propeller with guide vanes

At the tail of the helicopter is an airscrew pointing backwards, which provides extra power when the machine is flying forwards. Guide vanes are fitted behind the propeller which direct the airflow from the propeller to the side in order to compensate for the torque. However, the best known and most widely used method is:

Torque compensation by sideways acting tail propeller

Here an adjustable pitch propeller is arranged at 90° to the direction of flight at the tail of the helicopter. This propeller, known as the 'tail rotor', provides the required torque compensation. It can be set to match the demands of any flight situation by adjusting its pitch.

There is a drawback to all single rotor shaft drive systems: every time the flight situation alters, and every time the power output is varied, the torque compensation has to be altered precisely to match that change. In practice, this involves considerable extra demands on the pilot.

4. Multi-rotor helicopters

In the case of helicopters having more than one rotor, virtually 100% compensation for torque effect can be achieved by operating the rotors in opposite directions. The torque of the rotor revolving to the left will simply be counterbalanced by the torque of the other rotor turning to the right. The following basic systems have been developed:

Side rotors: The two rotors, turning in opposite directions, are arranged on the left and right hand side of the helicopter (Fig. 13).

Tandem rotors: The two rotors, also turning in opposite directions, are arranged one behind the other in the direction of flight (Fig. 14).

Intermeshing rotors: Here the shafts of the two side rotors are relatively close together, but they have a certain outward inclination, and are coupled in such a way that the rotor blades intermesh, without striking each other (Fig. 15).

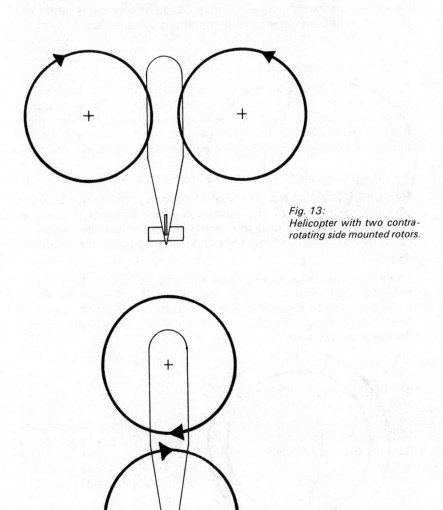

Fig. 13:
Helicopter with two contra-rotating side mounted rotors.

Fig. 14:
Helicopter with tandem rotors.

Coaxial rotors: The two contra-rotating rotors are arranged one above the other in this arrangement. The torque effects cancel each other out, and it is possible to eliminate altogether any auxiliary system of torque compensation by tail rotor etc. (Fig. 16).

The arrangements shown only illustrate the basic systems, amongst which an infinite number of rotor variations is possible.

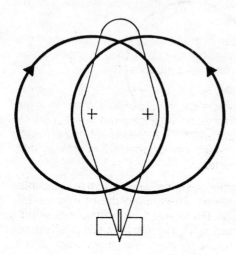

Fig. 15:
Helicopter with two inter-meshing rotors on canted axes.

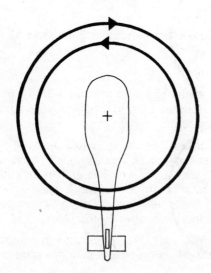

Fig. 16:
Helicopter with coaxial rotors (two rotors, one above the other).

However, all multi-rotor drive systems have the great disadvantage that the mechanical complication of the power system is very great, and the expense of providing more than one complete main rotor, complete with control system, is substantial. In addition, for a given motor performance, a single, large rotor is substantially more efficient than two or more correspondingly smaller rotors.

For these reasons, the arrangement of single rotor, shaft drive, and torque compensation via tail rotor, has found the widest acceptance in modern helicopter design.

In the model world this arrangement has also prevailed, and all the designs which have been successful to date utilize a shaft-driven main rotor, and a tail rotor for torque compensation.

This system is obviously easiest to resolve mechanically, and the adjustment of all the control systems is much simpler with a single rotor than with other types of drive system, or multi-rotor models. The problem of torque compensation by means of a tail rotor can be accepted, the more so since development has shown that this system can certainly be mastered.

This does not imply that other systems are not also possible, and may be feasible in Model terms. There is no doubt that a wide scope for experiment exists here. However, the explanations which follow are principally concerned with the most successful model helicopter system developed to date, using one main rotor and a tail rotor.

5. Producing the thrust

The vertical and horizontal thrust required for a helicopter to fly is produced by the main rotor alone.

The main rotor has two functions:

It has to provide the vertical thrust required to raise the machine from the ground and accelerate it upwards, and it also has to produce the thrust needed for horizontal flight.

As already explained, a helicopter, or rotary wing aircraft, has rotating wings or rotor blades instead of fixed wings. These are fixed at one end to a common rotor hub, which is in turn mounted on a revolving axle or main rotor shaft. A suitable power source transmits rotary movement to the main rotor shaft, which in turn rotates the entire rotor system like a horizontal propeller.

This rotation results in an airflow over the blades, and the combination of their special airfoil section and angle of incidence produces

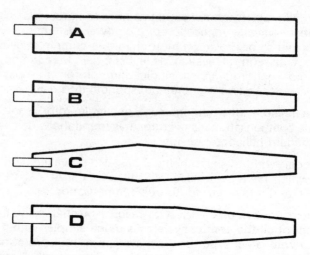

Fig. 17: Rotor blade designs:
A = parallel chord rotor blade   C = double tapered rotor blade
B = tapered rotor blade   D = parallel chord/tapered rotor blade

a lifting force in the same way as an aircraft wing.

The disadvantage here is that the rotor blades have a very high peripheral velocity and hence the rotor tips encounter a very powerful airflow, while the velocity of the airflow decreases steadily towards the hub.

The design of a rotor blade needs to be matched to these varying airflow speeds, and there are various possible methods of doing this, e.g. varying the airfoil, and varying the angle of attack of the rotor. In all cases the designer tries to ensure that each part of the blade is exactly matched to the speed of airflow at that point.

This demands relatively complex and, in production terms, expensive designs, made worse by the fact that each rotor blade has to withstand considerable bending loads, centrifugal loads and aerodynamic forces. For these reasons the design of a rotor blade always represents a compromise between the desirable and the technically feasible, with the result that there is a wide variation in design in the field of full-sized helicopters.

The universally accepted rotor blade design for the model helicopter features constant chord, uniform airfoil, and constant angle of incidence, along its whole length. However, washed-out blades are being tried, still constant chord but twisted to remove the angle of incidence towards the tips. Whether these blades are more efficient appears open to question.

In the model world, the two-bladed rotor, with its blades diametrically opposed, has been accepted more or less universally, owing to the simple rotor head design, easier setting up and the ease of balancing the blades which this layout affords.

Almost without exception rotor blade airfoils are fully symmetrical (Fig. 24). Earlier flat-bottomed lifting sections of the Clark Y type have virtually disappeared except perhaps in special cases where high lift is required, though even here an asymmetric double-convex airfoil is likely to be preferred.

6. Lift and drag of the rotor blade

I would need to write a lengthy, complicated treatise to cover in detail all the forces acting on the rotor. These include aerodynamic forces, which result in bending and twisting of the blade as well as providing lift, and various types of drag; they also include dynamic and centrifugal forces, bending moments, impact loads and so on.

We cannot afford to ignore these different forces, and for this reason they are covered in a later chapter, in connection with various corrective adjustments, balancing etc.

However, at this stage it will suffice to understand the principles of lift and drag, in isolation from other influences.

As shown in Fig. 18, the force produced by the airflow over a rotor blade (P) acts at a specific angle to the plane of rotation. This force can be divided into the lifting force (PA), which acts vertically, and the drag force (PW), acting in the horizontal plane, opposite to the direction of rotation. Lift (PA) can only be pro-

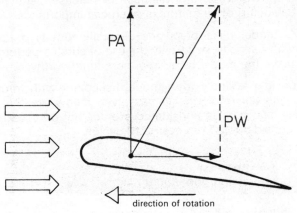

direction of rotation

Fig. 18: Total force P, lift force PA and drag force PW, acting on a rotor blade.

25

duced if the drag (PW) is overcome by a suitable power source. The ratio of PA:PW therefore determines the power required. PW is also one of the values which determines torque.

7. Power required

For full-size helicopters, power requirements are calculated on the basis of 0.15 to 0.20 BHP per kg. of the machine to be lifted, a figure which takes into account all the factors which reduce efficiency. This is known as the 'specific weight per unit power'. For example, a machine weighing 1000 kg would require a power of about 200 BHP at a specific weight per unit power of 0.2 BHP/kg. It should not be forgotten here that the thrust produced by the main rotor is reduced by the fuselage, tail, skids etc. being in the down-wash. These constitute what is known as 'harmful drag'.

It is also significant that the ratio of thrust to power increases as the rotor diameter increases, owing to the greater volume of air moved by the main rotor blades. The diameter of a main rotor system is, of course, limited for design reasons, and so we have to find an appropriate average value.

For model helicopters the values are similar to those in fullsize practice. A model helicopter of about 5 kg all-up weight, for example, can be powered by a motor producing about 1 BHP, with a considerable excess of power. Using one of today's modern 10 c.c. motors, which produce an average output of 1.3–1.5 BHP, a thrust of up to 10 kg can be achieved. This figure indicates a specific weight per unit power of 0.13 to 0.15 BHP/kg. This figure will also improve if the rotor diameter is increased, showing again that the balancing of all factors is of crucial importance.

In today's model helicopters one generally forfeits obtaining the maximum lift capacity, especially the use of surplus performance, in order to make the model faster and more flightworthy.

Let us consider a single rotor model helicopter with torque compensation via tail rotor; the values given below are the result of many tests, and can be considered average. Of course, the values will vary considerably from design to design.

Motor power as installed	100%
Tail rotor power absorption, about	18–20%
Cooling fan power absorption, about	15–18%
Mechanical losses, about	8–12%
Power at the rotor head, about	50–59%

26

These estimated figures show that around 50% of the motor's power output is absorbed by ancillaries or lost, leaving only about half of the motor performance available for effective lift impetus at the main rotor. Incorrectly adjusted main rotor blades can make the power balance even worse; a greater angle of incidence on the main rotor blades gives a greater torque, through which the power requirement to the tail rotor rises (mostly quite considerably). The result is a motor stall.

This estimate also shows that it is important to make all the essential sub-systems as efficient as possible. One tight bearing can be enough to soak up so much power from the motor that the remaining power is insufficient to sustain flight, or at least has a marked effect on the flight performance.

However, when the machine is moving forward, the rotating rotor system meets a headwind, and the rotor disc area then functions like an extra wing, or load-carrying area. The lift produced by the whole rotor system increases substantially when a certain forward speed is reached.

This is why two values are always stated for maximum height of a full-size helicopter: maximum in and outside ground effect, i.e. in hovering flight and forward flight.

8. Ground effect

The thrust of a rotor is also dependent on its distance from the ground. At a reasonable height, the air moved by the rotor is blown

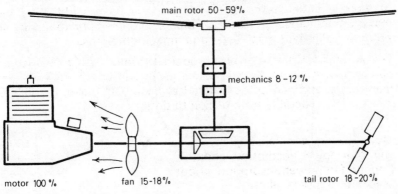

Fig. 19: Power absorption in a helicopter.

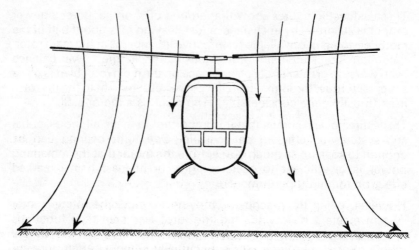

Fig. 20: Helicopter in ground effect.

directly downward, and to a large extent the rotor blades support themselves in a free-moving column of air.

Close to the ground, the air pushed downward by the rotor strikes the ground and pushes back upward to some extent. This effect is transferred to the main rotor, and produces extra thrust; this is known as 'ground effect'.

In practice, the result is that a helicopter needs less power to

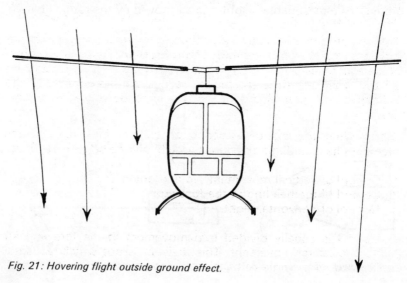

Fig. 21: Hovering flight outside ground effect.

28

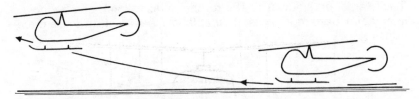

Fig. 22: Helicopter take-off in ground effect.

hover when it is close to the ground than when it is at height. If the available power is limited, the helicopter may be capable of flying within the confines of ground effect, but may not be capable of escaping from ground effect and climbing vertically.

This effect can be observed very clearly with models up to a rotor height of about 1 m, when flying a model of 1.5–1.6 m rotor diameter. An inadequately powered model may climb to a skid height of 10–20 cm in ground effect, but then be incapable of climbing higher vertically.

In such a case, the pilot can help the machine by allowing it to pick up forward speed in ground effect, and then exploit the additional airflow caused by forward flight.

9. Control functions

In contrast to a fixed wing aircraft, a helicopter can not only fly forwards, but can stay in one position in the air, fly sideways and backwards, fly vertically up and down, and rotate on its own axis.

This extreme manoeuvrability is the helicopter's great asset, but it does demand a more complex control system. Flying a helicopter is several times more complicated and difficult than controlling a fixed wing aircraft, since many movements and controls of the helicopter are interdependent, and have to be altered simultaneously.

Disregarding the interdependence of various functions for the moment, the main flight directions which have to be controlled are:

1. Control of vertical movement, up and down.
2. Control of the heading of the fuselage.
3. Control of horizontal flight.

Number 3 is usually divided into movement in the fore and aft plane and lateral movement. This division is not strictly accurate in the case of a single rotor, as the rotor itself has no 'forwards',

29

'backwards' or 'sideways'. The rotor is a disc which can be moved in any direction, regardless of what labels we attach to these directions.

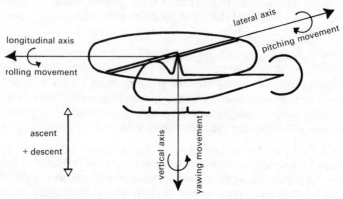

Fig. 23: The helicopter's principal axes and moments of rotation.

For this reason the horizontal control of the main rotor can only be stated with reference to the heading of the helicopter's fuselage. The direction in which the fuselage points determines the effective horizontal movement of the whole helicopter.

10. Vertical control by means of altering rotor speed

The simplest means of controlling a helicopter in the vertical plane is by changing the speed of rotation of the main rotor. The main rotor blades are fixed at a pre-determined angle of incidence, which is designed to provide maximum thrust when the motor is running at full throttle. Simply by altering the throttle setting, the motor's power can be reduced or increased to match the required degree of climb, hover, or descent.

This method of controlling vertical flight has proved ideal for model flight. Indeed, it was the only practical method for learning to fly helicopters at first; altering rotor speed via the throttle not only produced the degree of power needed for the manoeuvre being attempted, but also altered the speed of rotation of the tail rotor in direct relation to the speed of the main rotor. Once the tail rotor was trimmed, this function proved to be very easily controlled; this was tremendously welcome!

Another advantage of this method of control is that it is relatively straightforward mechanically. The rotor blades can be fixed more or less rigidly at the hub, and only need to be adjusted once. Control of thrust from then on is achieved via the motor throttle alone. Another good feature of this method of control is the acoustic feedback it provides; the exhaust note of the motor always corresponds to the thrust of the rotor, and the pilot soon learns to appreciate this.

The disadvantage of this method of vertical control is that every change of rotational speed takes a certain amount of time. This delay results in a time lag between the control input and the model's reaction. The pilot is forced to anticipate every move, taking the model's delayed reaction into account. This can be learned fairly quickly, and there are various ways of keeping the delay within reasonable limits.

It is particularly important to have a motor which is really controllable, and easy to adjust to its optimum setting. When the throttle is slowly opened, the motor's R.P.M. and power should gradually build up as the carburettor barrel rotates, and it should follow the stick movement just as smoothly when the throttle is closed. Not all motors and makes of carburettor fulfil these requirements, and therefore the matter of correct adjustment is of special importance.

Another important factor in achieving good controllability in vertical flight is the choice of suitable rotor diameter, rotor blades, and blade airfoils.

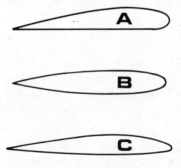

Fig. 24:
Typical blade sections used in model helicopters:
A = Clark Y
B = symmetrical section.
C = asymmetrical cambered profile.

For instance, lifting section rotor blades are usually used in rotor speed control systems, and such an airfoil produces a significant change in thrust with a relatively small change in speed of airflow (i.e. rotor speed). In practice, this means that only a small change of rotor speed is necessary to achieve a change in vertical movement. The delay between control input and reaction is reduced to a reasonable level in this way.

It is also important to try to keep the rotor blades as light as possible—

bearing in mind strength and rigidity—so that they can accept a change in rotor speed relatively quickly without undue inertia.

Another factor is that a change in rotor speed requires a certain force, which will be smaller if the rotor system is light and the resistance to speed change is small.

In other words: a heavy rotor system will present greater resistance to rotor speed changes; the delay will be correspondingly longer and the power required will be greater, resulting in higher torque for the length of time the change lasts. The increased torque has to be compensated for by the tail rotor, of course.

From the above explanation it is clear that the helicopter designer has a large number of interdependent factors to consider, and he has to find the best possible compromise. The many successful designs produced to date have proved that excellent results can be achieved, and there is no doubt that rotor speed control is technically the simplest, most robust and most trouble-free system (as far as adjustments are concerned) for vertical flight control.

In practice nowadays the simple throttle-controlled model is less often found, possibly because it permits only power-on flights and there is no auto-rotation should the engine cut. Nevertheless, the first successful model helicopter, my Bell Huey Cobra, was controlled in this way and, apart from the years of amusement it gave me, many people learned to fly with it. Today's beginners, however, demand collective pitch control, as described in the next section.

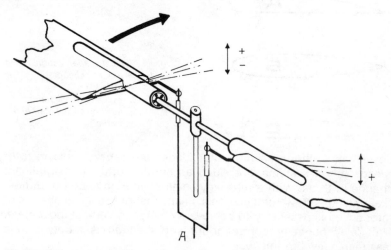

Fig. 25: Collective pitch control (simplified). By raising and lowering pushrod A, the pitch angle of both rotor blades is altered by the same amount (collectively).

11. Vertical control by means of collective pitch variation

In this system, the rotor blades are not rigidly fixed to the rotor head at a pre-determined angle of incidence.

The rotor head features 'feathering hinges' which make it possible to alter the angle of incidence of the rotor blades during flight.

Vertical movement is not controlled by altering the rotor speed; in fact the speed remains constant. Instead the angle of incidence of the rotor blades is varied simultaneously, or collectively. This results in an immediate change in rotor thrust, i.e. direct vertical control. This system is known as COLLECTIVE PITCH CONTROL.

This method of control is employed universally in full-size helicopters, partly for reasons of safety; if the motor should fail, the blades must be capable of a sort of 'gliding' position, which is termed 'auto-rotation'.

The undeniable advantage of collective pitch lies in the immediate control of vertical movement, avoiding the delays of the non-collective system. Vertical movements of just a few centimetres can be controlled precisely. If the air is very turbulent, sudden vertical movements can be corrected just as suddenly and directly.

But: The disadvantage of collective pitch for model helicopters is the much greater complexity of the rotor head and control system. The balancing of all the controls and the adjustment of all the pushrods etc. are considerably more difficult and complicated than in the case of rotor speed control.

There are many reasons for this:

The rotor head has to be equipped with feathering hinges which operate with absolute freedom under all conditions. This demands a relatively complicated rotor head.

The change in pitch of the rotor blades must occur evenly, i.e. collectively. This demands fully symmetrical, accurately adjusted blade control linkages.

The rotor blades must be finely balanced, and be identical aerodynamically, and their pitch must alter at exactly the same rate; all of which demands much greater care in the design of the rotor blades, as well as in their construction and fitting.

The motor has to be adjusted carefully, to ensure that the main rotor maintains the same speed under all conditions.

33

This factor is currently the critical point in the model sphere, as it has not proved possible to keep the rotor speed constant, or at least not completely. The current means of correcting this is to combine collective pitch control with motor throttle control in an attempt to open the throttle at the rate required to allow the rotor to maintain speed as the pitch of the blades is increased.

This is achieved either by means of a mechanical coupling of the two servos controlling 'throttle' and 'pitch' in the model or through an electronic mixture of both these functions through a special radio control system for helicopters.

In effect this means that a main rotor system with collective pitch control gives optimal value with regard to the speed of the vertical control, although there is still a need for precision in setting up.

This practice is exceedingly difficult, and is the real stumbling block in the use of the collective pitch system. The settings so painstakingly found and set can be upset by an alteration to the needle setting, a change of fuel or plug, different climatic conditions or altitude of the flying site, and considerable experience is needed to cope with these constant alterations.

Fig. 26: Rotor head with collective pitch from Schlüter model 'Heli Star'.

34

Experiments have been carried out with the aim of maintaining constant motor speed by electronic means, but as yet the results have not been satisfactory. The electronics are capable of instantly detecting a change in motor speed, and can send a correcting signal, but then the carburettor setting has to be altered, and the motor will then respond. This chain reaction takes so long that the 'constant speed' principle has been lost. In addition, every change in motor speed or collective pitch results in a change in torque, with the resultant torque reaction of the fuselage causing it to rotate around the vertical axis.

12. Control of fuselage heading

Here we are talking about the control of the fuselage's movements around its vertical axis, i.e. the direction in which the helicopter's fuselage is pointing. This is not synonymous with the direction in which the fuselage is flying, as this is a function of the main rotor alone, and is covered in the next chapter.

As previously described, the direction of the fuselage can be altered (torque compensation) by one of the following methods: a propeller mounted on the side of the fuselage, a jet of air blown out sideways from the tail of the fuselage, a tail propeller with adjustable

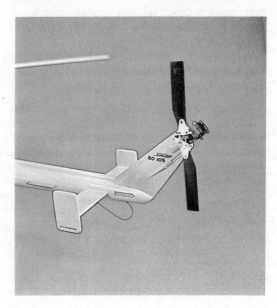

Fig. 27:
Typical tail rotor of a
model helicopter.
Schlüter 'BO 105' with
tail arm raised high.

35

vanes, or a variable pitch propeller mounted crosswise at the tail of the fuselage.

The last method is known simply as the 'tail rotor', and is used almost universally in full-size helicopters.

The same system has prevailed in the model world, and has proved ideal for our purposes. The tail rotor is virtually a perfectly normal propeller with adjustable pitch blades. In helicopter parlance we speak of 'collectively variable pitch tail rotor blades'.

Any change in heading therefore has to be controlled by the tail rotor, which is not too difficult in theory, provided that the influences on the tail rotor remain constant. Alas, that is very seldom the case, as the tail rotor is affected not only by the pitch of its blades, but also to a large extent by the speed of the main rotor, which varies according to load and conditions. These changes can be of quite a large order, and can make tail rotor control extremely difficult.

Here is an example:

The motor is running at a particular speed, and the main rotor and tail rotor at corresponding speeds. The model is hovering, and is now required to climb vertically. With collective pitch, the angle of incidence of the main rotor blades is increased. This results in a greater load on the motor, and as it cannot react instantly, the motor's speed falls. At the same time the increased load on the motor results in increased torque effect on the fuselage. The fuselage swings away from its original heading, and this is corrected with the tail rotor. Unfortunately, at this moment the rotational speed of the tail rotor drops.

With collective pitch, both increased torque and loss of rotor speed need to be controlled. Loss of rotor speed can be kept within reasonable limits by a combination of throttle and pitch adjustments but the increased torque has to be controlled by the tail rotor. This is relatively difficult, as the tail rotor control has to be matched to the pitch of the main rotor to provide 'tail rotor balance', so that a change of torque arising from a change of main rotor pitch is automatically accommodated by a corresponding alteration of tail rotor pitch. It is possible to achieve this by mechanical linkage of the respective pitch controls, but more elegant to do it electronically by means of a function mixer.

Electronic tail rotor control can also be achieved by the use of a gyro, and this is discussed in Section IV, para. 7(c).

In view of all these factors, control of the tail rotor deserves very special attention, and it is of the utmost importance that the pilot masters this control at the outset. Only when fuselage orientation is under complete control can the beginner think about controlling the main rotor system, or deliberately altering the direction of flight; these can only be thought of in relation to the fuselage.

13. Control of horizontal flight movement

A rotor system can be imagined as a disc or circular flat surface, which is known as the 'rotor disc'.

If this rotor disc rotates in the horizontal plane, the thrust produced by it acts exactly vertically. A helicopter would climb vertically in this situation.

If the disc is tilted to one side, an additional horizontal force is produced, acting in the direction of the tilt. The strength of the force depends on the angle of tilt. This horizontal force results in a constant acceleration of the helicopter in that direction.

The horizontal acceleration is maintained as long as the rotor disc is tilted, and provided that no braking effect is produced by air resistance, which increases as the speed rises.

If the disc were brought back to horizontal, the horizontal force would cease and the helicopter would continue moving in the same direction at constant speed, if air resistance did not provide a gentle, automatic braking action.

If the horizontal movement is to be stopped, the rotor disc system has to be tilted in the opposite direction.

The inclination of the rotor system to effect horizontal movement can be achieved in various ways:

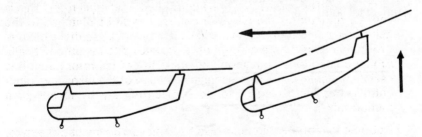

Fig. 28: Forward flight in a multi-rotor helicopter, by increasing lift on rear motor.

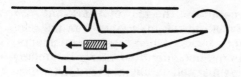

Multi-rotor helicopters are controlled by varying the thrust from each rotor. This inclines the whole machine, and with it the rotor discs, in the desired direction.

With single-rotor helicopters, the following methods are possible:

Centre of gravity shift control (Fig. 29)

The centre of gravity in the fuselage is shifted in order to incline the fuselage. This results in the rotor disc tilting. A variation on this is:

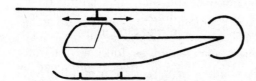

Fig. 30:
Rotor head shift control.

Rotor head shift control (Fig. 30)

Here the centre of gravity is altered by moving the rotor axis. In fact, both these systems are too unresponsive and complicated. Another possibility is:

Rotor head tilt control (Fig. 31)

The rotor head is mounted on the helicopter by means of a type of universal joint, i.e. it can be inclined in any direction to produce

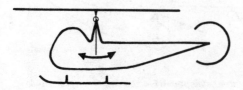

Fig. 31:
Rotor head tilt control.

38

movement in the required direction. In the full-size world this system is used principally for autogyros. It is not so suitable for helicopters, as the entire drive system has to be transmitted via the universal rotor suspension system, which would be technically very difficult, as well as involving unacceptably high control forces.

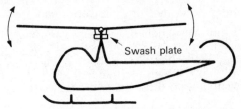

Fig. 32: Cyclic pitch control.

14. Cyclic pitch control

This system is used in virtually all full-size helicopters, and has also proved ideal for model purposes.

This method involves a certain amount of 'cheating', but it has absolutely nothing to do with gyroscopic forces, as so often mentioned in explanations of the system.

I say 'cheating' because the system involves a form of 'rotor head

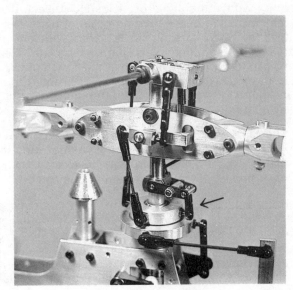

Fig. 33:
Swash plate of a model helicopter. The bar holds the outer 'fixed' ring and the inner is positioned by a cam on the main rotor shaft.

39

inclination', in which it is not the entire rotor head which tilts. In fact, the individual blades assume an angle of inclination which corresponds to the desired tilt of the rotor head.

To facilitate this action, the rotor blades are fixed to the rotor head in such a way that their angle of incidence can be varied independently from the rotor head.

The inclination of the rotor blades is achieved in most cases by means of the swash plate, a gimballed collar which rotates with the rotor system, and which can be tilted in any direction by the control system.

The variable pitch rotor blades are connected to the rotating part of the swash plate by a pushrod, and the angle of incidence of the blade varies from positive to negative according to the vertical movement of the collar.

For example, if the swash plate is exactly horizontal, and the rotor is exactly perpendicular to it, then the pitch of the rotor blades will remain constant, as the rotating collar of the swash plate does not move up or down during one revolution. The plane of the rotor disc remains constant relative to the fuselage.

If the swash plate is tilted, then the pitch of the individual blades will vary during each revolution, or cycle, with the same effect as if the whole rotor disc, or the whole helicopter, were tilted. In other words, the angle of incidence of each blade always follows the inclination of the rotating collar of the swash plate. This means that the pitch of each blade varies with one cycle according to the angle of inclination of the swash plate. The rotor system thus tries to follow the inclination of the swash plate by a cyclic variation in the pitch of the individual blades, until the rotor has the same inclination as the swashplate. In practice, this is the same as rotor inclination.

The helicopter's attitude in the air makes no difference here; for instance, if the helicopter is hovering with the swash plate at neutral, the rotor system will be exactly vertical, and will—disregarding wind effects—remain in one place.

If the swash plate is then tilted in a particular direction, then the rotor blades' pitch will vary cyclically during rotation, and they will take up the tilt of the swash plate after a certain delay. This involves an inclination of the entire rotor system compared with its previous position, and the result will be movement in the desired direction. In many cases collective pitch can also be varied by the

40

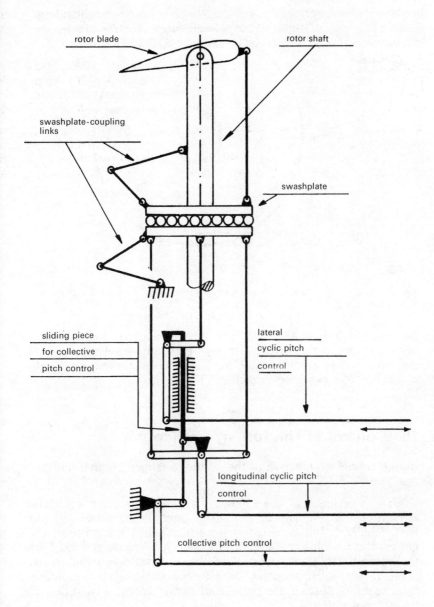

rotor blade

rotor shaft

swashplate-coupling
links

swashplate

sliding piece
for collective
pitch control

lateral
cyclic pitch
control

longitudinal cyclic pitch
control

collective pitch control

Fig. 34: System of cyclic and collective pitch control using a swashplate.

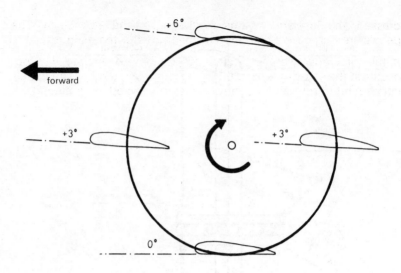

Fig. 35: Cyclic pitch control. The normal pitch angle is +3°. The swashplate is tilted 3° forward.

swash plate, independent of cyclic pitch change. This is achieved by allowing the swash plate to rise and fall independent of its inclination, thus automatically increasing or decreasing the angle of incidence of all the rotor blades.

15. Control of the full-size helicopter

Here is a brief explanation of the control arrangement in a full-size machine:

Vertical movement of the aircraft, i.e. collective pitch variation, is controlled by means of the blade pitch lever, known as the PITCH LEVER. This is usually on the pilot's left. Raising the lever causes the machine to climb, and lowering it causes the machine to descend. The pitch lever usually raises and lowers the swash plate. In smaller helicopters, which do not have fully automatic rotor speed regulation, the pitch lever often features a twist grip to control motor output.

Control over the fuselage heading, i.e. rotation about its vertical axis, is achieved via foot pedals, which operate the variable pitch tail rotor to provide torque compensation. If the right pedal is depressed, the fuselage swings to the right, and vice versa. The pedals are also used to counteract the torque of the main rotor.

If the pilot operates the pitch lever, he has to operate the foot pedals at the same time to counter the change in torque. The pedals correspond to the rudder control system in a fixed wing aircraft.

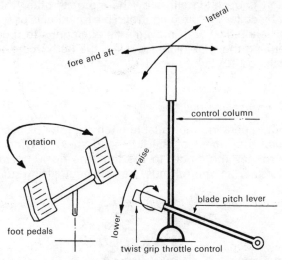

Fig. 36: Arrangement of controls in a full-size helicopter.

Horizontal flight movements are controlled by the central control column, which can also be compared with the control column of a fixed wing aircraft. In a single rotor helicopter, the column tilts the swash plate, thus altering cyclic pitch. The rotor plane takes up the same inclination, and the result is flight in the desired direction. Pushing the column forward inclines the machine forwards, and forward flight results. Pulling the column back results in backwards flight. Moving the column to one side results in sideways flight etc.; it is obvious that flight in any horizontal direction is possible.

The pilot of a full-size helicopter clearly has 'both feet and both hands full'.

16. Control arrangements for the model helicopter

The model pilot also has his hands full, even more so than the full-size pilot, as he has to control the tail rotor with his hands, and not his feet.

Radio-controlled model helicopters are controlled by a total of four functions, two on each stick.

A. Climb and descent

This function is operated either by the motor throttle (rotor speed control) or by collective pitch control. This function is best operated by the left hand stick, with movements analogous to those of the full-size: pulling the stick back (towards the body) corresponds to 'climb', pushing the stick forward—'descend'.

B. Control of fuselage heading

This function, operating the variable pitch tail rotor, is best controlled by lateral movement of the left-hand stick. Moving the stick to the left rotates the model to the left (the nose, not the tail!), and vice versa. This control must be self-neutralising, to facilitate

Fig. 37:
Pilot's seating position in a full-size helicopter (Hughes 300).

trimming for hovering flight. This control corresponds to the full-size helicopter's foot pedals.

C. Control in the horizontal plane

This function operates via the swashplate to provide cyclic pitch variation. Two functions are required, usually controlled by the right hand stick. Moving the stick fore and aft corresponds to fore and aft inclination of the swash plate, while moving it from side to side results in a corresponding inclination to either side. Between these four extremes all possible horizontal directions are available. For technical reasons this control is operated by two functions (longitudinal and lateral), but in practice this can be considered a single control, i.e. horizontal movement in the direction of stick movement. Here too the stick should be self-neutralising, so that stationary hovering flight can be trimmed 'hands off'. This control corresponds to the full-size helicopter's control column.

The control arrangement described here is by no means the only possibility, nor is it the undisputed favourite. However, I consider it to be the most logical, as it is closest to full-size practice. There are alternative arrangements which have also proved entirely practical.

These comments apply particularly to pilots who already fly fixed wing R/C aircraft, who have learned certain reflex actions. In their case, the tail rotor control should take the place of the rudder, and lateral cyclic pitch that of the ailerons; more on this under installation of the R/C system.

17. Rotor suspensions

As in full-size machines, various methods of fixing the rotor head to the fuselage are employed, all of which have their good and bad points; here we concentrate on their applications in the model sphere.

A. Fully articulated suspension

The rotor system is connected to the drive shaft by fully articulated suspension, allowing it to move freely without transferring motion to the drive shaft and thus the helicopter itself. The pivot allowing the whole system to rock is called the hinge and the pivot line across the blade, allowing the tips to rise and fall independently, is the flapping hinge. With two rotor blades directly opposite a joint flapping hinge can be used through a connector called the see-saw. This averages the flight loads of the blades without transferring them to the flapping hinges and therefore to the main shaft and the fuselage (Fig. 39).

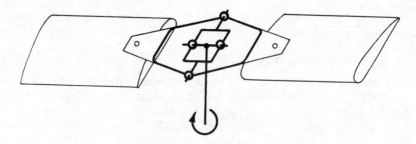

Fig. 38: Fully articulated rotor blade suspension.

This method of suspension provides excellent smoothness in the whole rotor system, as it is not affected by any fuselage movements. Even gusts of wind have no effect, and the controls operate very smoothly and gently. The drawback is that the controls are less responsive, as the fuselage does not immediately follow the inclination of the rotor system. It only reacts to acceleration or retardation in a horizontal direction after such movements have been initiated. The result is delayed response to the controls to a greater or lesser extent.

B. Suspension with individual flapping hinges

In this arrangement each blade has its own flapping hinge and connection to a see-saw is omitted. Each blade can thus move independently of the other(s) so that a particular flight load on one blade is not averaged out over the other(s). Blade loads tend to be transferred to the drive shaft and thus to the fuselage, via the hub, and the greater the distance of the hinge lines from the hub centre (see X in Fig. 40) the more pronounced is the force transference.

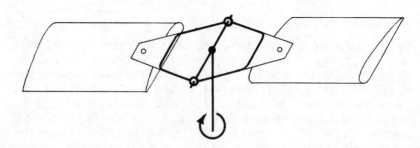

Fig. 39: Hinged rotor blade mounting, combined flapping hinges.

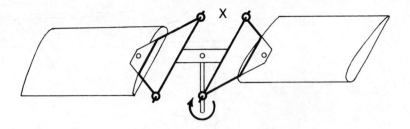

Fig. 40: Semi-rigid blade suspension with individual flapping hinges.

C. Damped suspension

This is effectively the arrangement shown in Fig. 39 but with dampers limiting the free movement of the see-saw. Part of the blade load is thus transferred to the drive shaft and fuselage: the harder the dampers the stronger will be the influence of the blades on the fuselage.

C. Rigid suspension

Here the rotor system is allowed no free movement; it is virtually rigidly fixed to the rotor shaft, and thence to the fuselage. However, the word 'rigid' should not be taken literally, as there is always a degree of flexibility in the rotor shaft, the rotor head, the blade suspension and the blade itself. The term 'non-hinged suspension' is really closer to the truth.

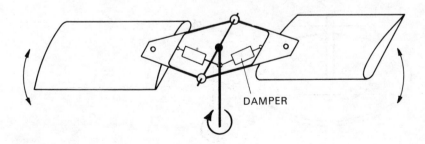

DAMPER

Fig. 41: Hinged rotor blade mounting with dampers.

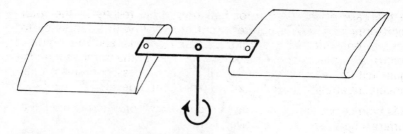

Fig. 42: Rigid rotor blade suspension (not hinged).

The effect of this rotor head is that every control movement, that is every position change of the rotor disc, is immediately transmitted to the rotor shaft and the fuselage. The usual expression is a high 'Rotormast Element'. With remote control helicopters this means that one can learn a control movement and also the fuselage movement immediately.

However, the rigid or non-hinged rotor head has one major, crucial disadvantage when applied to models: it tends to intensify vibration in the whole machine, and can even lead to completely uncontrollable oscillation. The reason for this is what is known as 'gyroscopic precession', a particular characteristic of a gyroscope which is exploited in gyroscopic control systems, but which is very harmful here.

This characteristic works as follows: a gyroscope—and the rotating rotor is one effectively—presents considerable resistance to a force which tries to incline it in a given direction, and instead of moving in that direction, it will try to move in a direction exactly 90° to that desired.

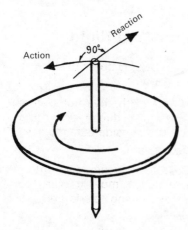

Fig. 43:
System of gyroscopic precession.

In the case of the rigid rotor helicopter, this results in the rotor shaft opposing, say, a control input 'forward' with a tendency to move to one side. As it is rigid, it cannot do this, and this rigidity creates a further gyroscopic effect, to which the rotor responds again with a reaction offset by 90°. This process continues, one movement amplifying the next, and oscillation develops.

This type of oscillation can set in during flight, or after the machine suffers a hard 'arrival' or skewed landing.

Usually the oscillation can be interrupted by a radical change in rotor speed, or by steering the model strongly to one side, but sometimes such action compounds the problem, leading to a mechanical failure or a crash.

Here too the designer's brief is to seek out a workable compromise between the positive and the negative factors.

Almost without exception model helicopters with two rotor blades have a mixture of a joined see-saw and joined flapping hinge with damping of the hinge movement. How strong the damper should be will differ with the use and adjustments and personal view of the pilot and the desired flying qualities of the model. Soft dampers give a quieter, smoother rotor run, whereby the fuselage follows the rotor movement (pitch of the rotor disc) gently. Hasty movements of the rotor, through controls or bad weather for example, will be contained by the dampers and will not be transferred.

For competition flying the dampers are often very hard, giving greater steering power with immediate response of the fuselage and easier control in gusts of wind. It is possible to arrange good rigid suspension which in the middle zone allows sufficient play for the feared pitching to be avoided.

18. Asymmetrical airflow in forward flight

All the foregoing explanations and statements only apply to stationary hovering flight, or vertical climb and descent.

However, if the helicopter flies in a horizontal path, the rotor system will be influenced by the flow of air past it in one direction, and the effects increase as speed rises. The result is a considerable increase in the loads on the whole control system.

The rotor blade which is moving *into* the airstream encounters a much faster airflow than the blade which is moving *with* the airstream. The terms used here are the 'advancing' blade and the 'retreating' blade.

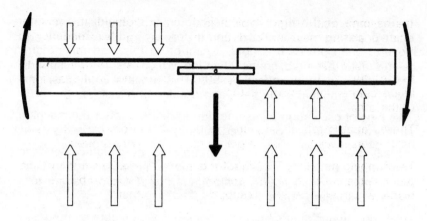

Fig. 44: Asymmetrical airflow of a rotor system in forward flight.

In the case of the advancing blade, the airstream is added to the normal airflow over the blade, and the aerodynamic lift produced increases. For the retreating blade, the airstream reduces the airflow, and lift is reduced.

Depending on the direction of rotation of the rotor, the advancing blade will always produce more lift than the retreating blade, the difference being a function of flying speed.

Rotors spinning at high speed are affected less by this than slower rotors, as in the latter case the airflow from the airstream is a greater proportion of the rotor's own speed. The result of this asymmetrical distribution of lift is a rolling tendency towards the side of the retreating blade, which can lead to a severe bank developing, and even to the machine turning over, and for this reason with model helicopters today the tendency is towards faster rotor rotation.

19. Flapping hinges—lead/lag hinges

Flapping hinges are fitted to lessen the variation in lift between the advancing and retreating blades, and especially to prevent the resulting rolling tendency reaching the fuselage. In full-size machines the main purpose of the hinges is to avoid the considerable extra load on the blade connections (see also Rotor Suspensions, 17).

'Flapping' in helicopter terms means the vertical up and down movements of individual rotor blades. When the rotor encounters

50

the asymmetrical airflow typical of forward flight, the advancing blade is able to move upward, and the retreating blade downward.

A flapping hinge allows each blade to move up or down according to the transient forces acting upon it, without unduly stressing the blade connection, affecting the helicopter, or transmitting effects to the other blades.

These flapping movements are clearly audible from many types of helicopters, especially the larger types with only two blades.

The flapping hinge allows the rotor blade to swing upward, and this prompts the question: what happens to the lift produced by the rotor blade, which is supposed to support the helicopter?

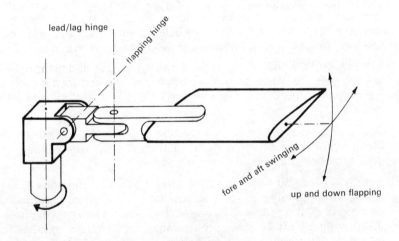

Fig. 45: Flapping hinge and lead/lag hinge of a rotor blade.

It has to be borne in mind here that the main rotor blades are subject to a powerful centrifugal force as a result of their fast rotational speed; this force keeps the blades in a virtually horizontal position, or more accurately, at right angles to the main rotor shaft. The only force opposing this radial 'stretching' effect is the lift force acting upwards, and this force is many times smaller in magnitude than the centrifugal force.

These opposing forces produce a degree of 'dihedral' in the rotor blades, known as the 'coning angle'. More on this in chapter III.

In model helicopters with two rotor blades and a semi-rigid rotor suspension, a flapping hinge system is already built in to all intents, working on both blades at once. The asymmetrical effect of the air-stream is roughly of equal magnitude on the advancing and the retreating blades. As the two blades are diametrically opposed, the one blade swings upward by exactly the same amount as the other swings downward.

The 'flapping' of the rotor blades also results in a tendency for the blade to move in the direction of rotation. This is a result of what are known as *Coriolis forces*.

The centre of gravity of a blade tends to maintain a constant speed. As the blade flaps, the centre of gravity approaches the rotor's central axis, with the result that the blade tends to speed up around the rotor's axis. In fact, it is trying to advance past its original position, and this tendency is known as 'blade lead' in helicopter terminology. This is why full-size helicopters often have additional lead/lag hinges, which allow the rotor blades to move in the direction of rotation.

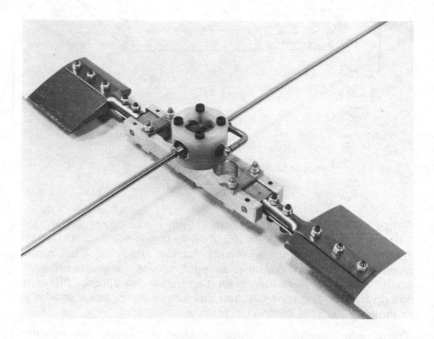

Fig. 46: Typical model rotor with flapping hinges (Gazelle standard).

In the model field the lead/lag hinge has not proved to be essential, as the flapping movements stay within reasonable limits. Nevertheless, these factors do exist and they can distort the blade holder or push it round in the direction of rotation, especially if the rotor is subjected to heavy loads or high speeds. In many constructions today normal rotor blade stabilisers on a forked blade connection with only one screw are produced, which automatically gives a form of lead hinge which will be effective under extreme loads.

Phase angle

To avoid unnecessarily large flapping movements, and to lessen the rolling moment which results from the asymmetrical airflow encountered during forward flight, what is known as a delta hinge is employed.

This involves an automatic reduction in blade pitch when it flaps upwards, and an increase in pitch when it flaps downwards. A considerable damping effect on the flapping movement results from this.

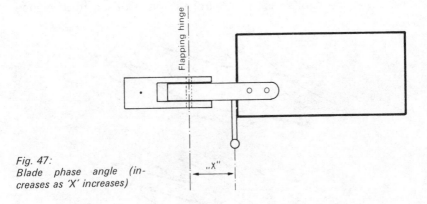

Fig. 47:
Blade phase angle (increases as 'X' increases)

The effect can be achieved by displacing the blade pitch change connections away from the axis of the flapping motion, or by setting the flapping hinge axis at an angle, which, if properly set up, can allow a certain amount of lead/lag movement.

This effect has not been exploited in the model area, as it is usually difficult to control accurately, and can reduce controllability, but in some special cases the system might be feasible.

20. Auto-rotation

This term refers to the unpowered gliding flight of a helicopter. The rotor blades continue turning, despite the lack of power, in the manner of a windmill, and produce some lift. Auto-rotation is vital to the full-size helicopter pilot if he suffers motor failure.

The crucial point in auto-rotation is that the rotor must continue rotating after the motor has stopped. Only then can the aircraft 'glide' and remain controllable.

It can be shown mathematically that when the rotating rotor encounters an airflow of a certain speed the airflow stops slowing the rotor, and actually drives it, allowing rotor speed to be maintained.

The easiest way of understanding auto-rotation is to compare it with the gliding flight of a sailplane. Such an aircraft glides, driven by its weight, at a certain downward angle, and is supported by the lift produced by its wings. The pilot's task is to control the angle of descent of the aircraft, and therefore the airflow over the wings, so that the shallowest possible glide angle is achieved.

Practically the same process occurs during auto-rotation. In this case it is the pilot's task to control the pitch of the rotor blades

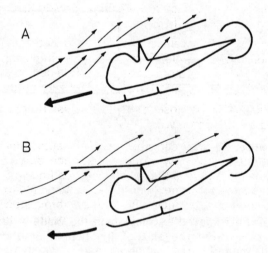

Fig. 48: Auto-rotation:
A. The rotor blades are in the 'glide' setting, the fuselage is inclined forward by pushing the stick forward, and the rotor blades meet an upward airflow.
B. By pulling back the stick the nose rises to flare out, the rotor is supported by the airflow, forward speed and sinking speed are reduced.

(instead of the wings) to ensure that the blades continue rotating. This would correspond to a steep glide in a fixed wing aircraft. The 'glide' therefore takes the form of tight spirals around the rotor head. If the pitch of the blades is increased, the 'glide' and therefore the rotor speed will slow down, and vice versa.

In practice, if the helicopter's engine fails, the pilot immediately changes the blades' pitch from the relatively large angle needed for powered flight to a very small angle, in order to enter the glide phase, i.e. to keep the rotor speed up. This is done with the pitch lever. The drive system is also disengaged, so that the mechanics of the rotor system do not brake the rotor unnecessarily. The pilot will even try to raise the rotor speed further by another reduction in pitch, so that a certain amount of kinetic energy is 'in reserve' in the rotor system for a flare out at landing. This is analogous to the fixed wing aircraft's high speed approach and flare out.

The old rule of 'Speed is half the battle' could be applied equally to the helicopter: 'Rotor speed is half the battle'.

As previously pointed out, rotor lift is increased substantially by the greater airflow encountered in forward flight, and for this reason the helicopter pilot tries to keep up a good forward speed when in auto-rotation, apart from maintaining rotor speed.

To achieve this he has to push the machine forward as it glides by pushing the control column forward.

If the rotor speed is maintained correctly and if the machine is kept at the ideal glide angle, it can show a surprisingly good glide and if enough reserve rotor speed is maintained, it is possible to flare out for the landing, and touch down at zero ground speed.

Our saying would really be closer to the truth thus: 'Rotor speed and forward speed are the battle won'.

Model helicopters can also carry out excellent auto-rotation, provided that the pilot learns how to judge the touch-down correctly. The basic requirement here is the installation of a freewheel device, and it has proved best to fit the freewheel directly on the rotor shaft. All the drive components, including the tail rotor, stop rotating when the motor stops, and only the main rotor continues turning.

21. Dangerous flight phases

It must be understood that there are situations in which it is not possible to enter auto-rotation and carry out an unpowered landing. These danger situations exist for all helicopters, and the phases are laid down individually for each design of full-size machine.

Basically there are two 'danger situations. One is at high speed close to the ground, and the other is stationary hovering flight at zero forward speed. These critical phases exist for model helicopters in a similar form, and they should be avoided as far as possible.

A further area of danger is the machine's own rotor blast. This downward directed stream of air, known as the 'downwash', is caused by the rotor blades, which pull a certain volume of air through the rotor disc, push it downwards, and produce lift as the opposite

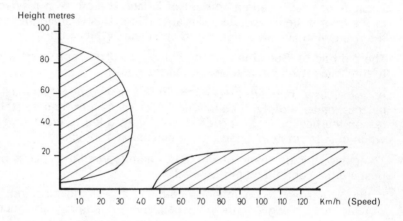

Fig. 49: Example of dangerous phases of flight (shaded).

reaction. (We have mentioned this already under 'ground effect') As long as the down-wash is able to flow downwards freely, the aerodynamic forces on the rotor system remain constant.

This does not apply, however, if the helicopter loses height quickly in a vertical descent. In doing so it can strike its own downwash and this reduces lift considerably. The descent accelerates, and the effect becomes more and more pronounced. The machine is 'flying' in its own downwash.

This dangerous fast vertical descent must be avoided at all costs. If the helicopter should get into this situation, a stall can only be avoided by the pilot pushing his machine forward out of the downwash. Immediately the effect will vanish. It is not for nothing that full-size pilots speak of 'lowering yourself gently'.

The model helicopter suffers exactly the same effect, and it is one situation that the beginner will find a problem. It is particularly difficult to judge the rate of descent when the model is more or less directly above the pilot, and sometimes he will notice too late that the model is descending too fast, and hitting its own downwash. There is only one escape route: forward cyclic, and fly out of the downwash.

22. Helicopter stability

In our discussions so far on the flying characteristics of helicopters and the methods of control used, the matters of stability and behaviour in flight have not been mentioned.

It is a common assumption that the helicopter's layout means that it is to some extent hanging beneath its revolving rotor rather like a parachute, and will swing back to the vertical after being disturbed; it is thus 'stable'. This is not the case.

Here we need to define the different types of 'stability' as related to helicopters.

1. 'stable' means that the effect of any disturbance ceases when the cause of the disturbance is removed, and the original situation is restored.

2. 'neutrally stable' means that the effect of any disturbance remains constant, and when the cause of the disturbance is removed, the situation remains the same.

3. 'unstable' means that the effect of any disturbance increases when the cause of the disturbance is removed.

According to these definitions, a helicopter is at best 'neutrally stable', and more likely to be 'unstable'.

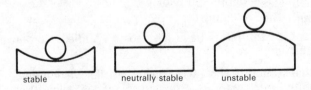

Fig. 50: Concepts of 'stability'.

This is quite obvious; for example, a hovering helicopter is not subject to any influences which try to maintain its position, or which try to return it to its original position after it has been disturbed. To the helicopter it makes no difference whether it is flying here, 10m away, or 100m away. Nothing is trying to bring it back to the place from which it started.

As the rotor is circular (in effect), there is no relevant concept of 'front' or 'rear' to assist in orientation. For this reason there is no preferred direction for the helicopter to take up when it flies away from its take-off point.

We can see that the idea of 'stability' is really superfluous in helicopter terms; we should really be discussing 'neutral stability'.

It follows then that all the efforts aimed at making a helicopter 'stable' are really aimed at designing a machine as 'neutrally stable' as possible, i.e. the helicopter should maintain a given flight situation or direction as long as possible, without deviating from it. The most important aim, however, is that it must not intensify any movement of its own accord.

Assuming that no special stabilising equipment is fitted, there are some basic factors which contribute to what we call 'stability'.

1. Low rotor loading, analogous to low wing loading.

2. A small angle of incidence for the rotor blades, i.e. low aerodynamic loading on the rotor blades.

3. Heavy rotor blades, i.e. relatively unresponsive behaviour of the whole rotor system.

4. A large distance between the flapping hinges, i.e. the most direct transmission of the rotor blade forces to the rotor hub, to damp down fuselage movements (the rigid rotor represents the maximum here).

It is possible to 'design in' a high degree of 'stability', or perhaps we should say to reduce the 'instability' to an acceptable level, which is manageable by the pilot.

Most full-size helicopters are not fitted with special stabilising equipment, as the pilots have learned to handle a certain amount of 'instability'.

Older helicopters, and especially smaller machines, usually incorporated extra stabilising devices, as these designs' size meant that they needed to have too little inherent stability. In any case, the aim was to make the task of piloting as easy as possible.

Model helicopters also incorporate stabilising aids, to make control easier for the pilot. There are models without stabilisers, but they are not exactly easy to learn to fly.

Almost all stabilising systems are based on the principle that a gimballed gyroscope system tends to maintain its position, even when its drive axis is altered.

In a helicopter, this manifests itself in a universally mounted 'gyroscope' on the main rotor shaft, consisting of a long rod (stabiliser bar, or flybar) with weights mounted on the ends. This gyroscope system rotates with the main rotor, and maintains its position in space, even when the helicopter starts to move, e.g. when inclined forwards. This 'inertia' of the stabiliser system is used to control or damp down movements of the main rotor system.

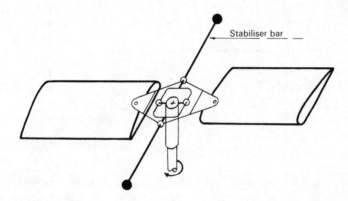

Stabiliser bar

Fig. 51: Stabiliser bar on a fully articulated rotor without control or damping systems.

23. The BELL stabilising system

In this stabilising system, a stabiliser bar with tip weights is mounted on the rotor head, as just described. The system is connected via a series of levers to the main rotor blade pitch change levers.

If the helicopter tilts over, the stabiliser bar maintains its position in space, and does not follow the tilt. Simultaneously it steadies the main rotor blades, via the system of levers, so that they also maintain their original course, and also resist the tilt.

This 'original' position cannot be allowed to be maintained indefinitely; the main rotor system must also be under the control of the pilot. Hence the main rotor blades can be controlled independently of the stabiliser.

The disadvantage of this method of control is that the stabilising system does not follow an intentional inclination of the helicopter, and thus hinders proper control.

To counter this effect, 'dampers' are fitted which force the stabiliser bar to follow an inclination of the helicopter. This deliberate stabiliser damping makes the machine controllable.

It is vital that these dampers are set correctly, and for this reason

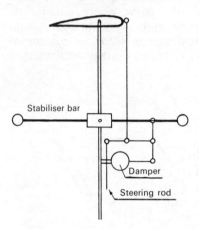

Fig. 52:
'Bell' system of stabilisation and damping.

very precise instructions for adjustment are given by BELL for their machines, as the settings have a very critical effect on the handling of the machine.

Many variants of the BELL system have been tried in the model field, but the correct amount of damping has proved an obstacle to success. The only successful version has been a variation on the BELL system using an aerodynamic form of damping—as in the HILLER system.

24. The HILLER stabilising system

Here a second, 'servo rotor' is utilized to control and influence the main rotor. This servo rotor also acts as a stabilising gyroscope system, but the rotating weights consist of small, airfoil section wings, known as 'control paddles' or 'servo paddles'.

These paddles can be controlled cyclically, just like the main rotor blades, via the swash plate. If the control paddles' setting is not altered, they act purely as stabiliser weights, and maintain their position in space, thus holding the stabiliser bar stationary. If the paddles are subjected to a cyclic pitch command via the swash plate, their position in space alters, for the period of the command. If the cyclic command is removed, the paddles act once more as stabilisers in their new position in space.

This servo rotor is connected to the main rotor by a rod, and transmits its movements directly to the main rotor blades. The result is a system of direct stabilisation and indirect control of the main rotor.

Another effect of the servo paddles is that the stabilising system follows any inclination of the helicopter after a certain amount of delay, thus achieving to some extent an aerodynamic post-control effect The result is relatively good stability, combined with good controllability, with the sole limitation that there is always a slight delay between the control input and the reaction: the servo rotor is controlled first, which then adjusts the main rotor. This delay is easily mastered and proves to be no problem in practice. One particular advantage is that the delay remains the same, and does not vary according to the setting of the dampers or other mechanical fittings.

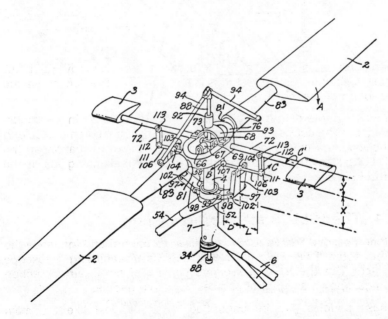

Fig. 53: The original 'Hiller' control system, with separate and individually controlled stabiliser bars (from Hiller patent, March 1953).

The Hiller control system is best suited to model helicopter use, as it requires no mechanical damper. The servo rotor also requires much less power to control than would direct control of the main rotor blades.

The original Hiller system does require modification for model use. For example, the control paddles are attached to separate arms, which are mounted on the main rotor and controlled independently. All the control forces and centrifugal forces act on these mountings, and this is not really practical in model terms without incurring great expense in bearings etc.

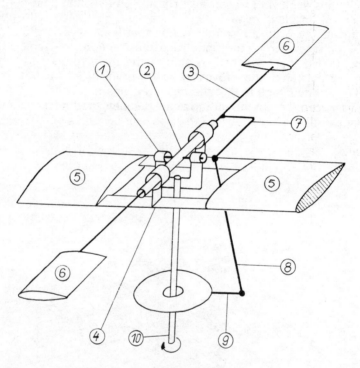

Fig. 54: Simplified 'Schlüter' rotor head based on the Hiller system, but with a single, one-piece stabiliser bar and a single control pushrod (diagrammatic view of system from the patent application).

1=rotor hub
2=universal joint cross-piece with
    hollow cross-shaft
3=one-piece stabiliser bar
4=see-saw
5=blades

6=Hiller type control paddles
7=control arm
8=one single control pushrod
9=swashplate
10=rotor shaft

The original Hiller system also requires connecting rods between the control paddles and arms, and this is complicated further by the control linkages for collective pitch control. The Hiller system in any case requires individual feathering hinges for the main rotor blades.

25. The SCHLÜTER rotor

In 1969–70 the Schlüter rotor was developed, retaining the control paddles typical of the Hiller system, and it represents a simplification of the Hiller design for model use.

An important feature is the one-piece stabiliser bar, which runs through the centre of the gimballed blade suspension and has control paddles on its ends. The centrifugal forces are cancelled out within the one-piece stabiliser bar, and therefore no loads are placed on the system or the mounting. At the same time all the connecting rods are eliminated, as the control paddles are directly connected by the stabiliser bar.

Cyclic control of the servo paddles does not need separate rods to the paddles; simply rotating the stabiliser bar adjusts both wings by an equal amount. Only one pushrod is needed to rotate the stabiliser bar, and this constitutes another typical feature of the Schlüter rotor, in addition to the one-piece stabiliser bar.

The simplification of the control system to a single rod, the successful solution to the problem of operating the one-piece stabiliser bar, in conjunction with the Hiller principle, and the other major

Fig. 55:
The original, but technically simplified 'Schlüter' rotor on the 'Heli-Baby' helicopter.

Fig. 56A: The first 'Schlüter' rotor of early 1970 on the 'Bell Huey Cobra'.

Fig. 56B: Rotor head using the same system, but with flapping hinges (D-S 22 and 'Gazelle').

64

simplifications, eventually resulted in success. By late 1969 and early 1970, the first controlled flights with a radio-controlled model helicopter were carried out all over the world. In due course the vital features of the Schlüter rotor were patented.

The system was again simplified by mounting the one-piece, rotating stabiliser bar on a fully articulated main rotor. This meant that all stabilising and control movements were transmitted directly from the stabiliser bar to the main rotor blades without any transmission components.

The main rotor blades for their part are rigidly connected via a common bridge piece, known as the 'see-saw', in the centre of the rotor. They have a constant angle of incidence. This system eliminates all the technical complications of the rotor head. Thrust is controlled by changing rotor speed.

The Schlüter 'Expert' rotor represents a variation on this rotor system. It also features a one-piece stabiliser bar, but instead of being connected to a rigid see-saw, it is connected to the control arms of the individual blade pitch change axles. Cyclic blade control is achieved by the Hiller system, while simultaneous raising and lowering provides collective pitch control.

26. Combination rotor systems

There are many combinations of the well known Bell and Hiller systems, which have resulted from practical experience with these rotor heads.

The first variation is to fit Hiller type control paddles to a Bell system head instead of the stabiliser weights, using no dampers. If the helicopter tilts, the stabiliser bar tilts with it, and the paddles fitted to it have a sort of post-control effect on the stabilising system. The drawback is that this system's post-control effect is limited, and a machine fitted with it can be impossible to recover from extreme situations.

Another derivative is to use Hiller paddles on the Bell system as before, plus cyclic control of the paddles as well as the main rotor blades. This provides more or less direct control of the main rotor blades à la Bell, and also control of stabilisation à la Hiller.

Almost without exception, today's modern helicopters are fitted with so-called combination systems of Bell & Hiller and have the continuous Schlüter stabiliser bar. More of this in IV/10.

RCHM—C

III. The rotor blades and their dynamics

1. The forces acting on the rotor blade

The design, construction and balancing of the rotor blades have a very important influence on the smoothness of running of the rotor system, and in particular on the subsequent stability and controllability of the whole helicopter. The forces transmitted via the pushrods to the servos can be very considerable, and must not be underestimated, as they are often the reason for loss of control.

To understand the interdependence of these forces, and to be able to sort out problems, we need to separate the different forces produced by the rotor blades. As the following explanations will show, we are not only discussing the forces produced by the blade as it rotates, but also the various types of forces exerted on the rotor blades by the air. These are superimposed on other forces, and it is often difficult to be exactly clear where this or that load is coming from.

Basically, we can differentiate between:

a)   static forces,

b)   dynamic forces,

c)   aerodynamic forces.

The static forces a) are produced when the rotor is stationary; they can easily be measured and balanced out.

The dynamic forces b) arise during rotation of the rotor system. They are not easily understood, although the most important components can be corrected when checking the static forces.

The aerodynamic forces c) only arise as a result of the influence of the air on the rotor blades when the rotor system is rotating.

The resultant aerodynamic forces cannot really be measured using modelling equipment, and can only be estimated by a combination of calculation and comparative experiment.

2. The static forces

This term covers all the forces which arise without the influence of rotation. It basically involves balancing the main rotor blades, and achieving static balance. This is explained in fig. 57.

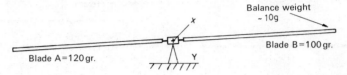

Fig. 57

A rotor head is mounted with its main rotor shaft X on support Y. We will assume zero friction. The two rotor blades are fixed to the rotor head, and set in a perfectly straight line (!). The only difference: blade A, at 120g, is heavier than blade B at 100g.

Blade A will pull the whole rotor down. The logical solution is to ballast blade B. The question is—where to attach the weight?

Statically speaking, i.e. disregarding the forces arising later during rotation, it would suffice to make blade B heavier by 10g at its tip, shown in the diagram by the arrow. The rotor system would now balance about axis X and be statically balanced.

But: Blade B still only weighs 110g (100+10g) and therefore is 10g lighter than blade A. Nevertheless, purely static balance has been achieved.

3. The dynamic forces

Let us stay with the previous example: it can be shown mathematically (see chapter IX: calculations and formulae), that the 120g. blade A produces the same centrifugal forces as the 110g blade B with its tip weight of 10g. Without going into the mathematics, the reason is simply that the 10g weight on the blade tip travels much faster, or rotates much faster around the rotor axis, than the remainder of the blade, and therefore the greater flywheel effect of this blade (B) counteracts its lower total weight (see Fig. 58). It is clear then that blade A (120g) is dynamically exactly balanced by blade B (110g) when rotated around axis X. However, this is only true if the blades are exactly in line, i.e. the radial forces arising from centrifugal force are acting directly through the pivot, or centre point, X.

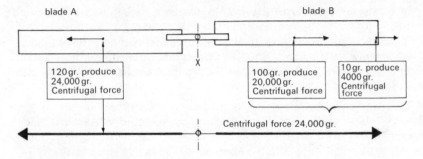

Fig. 58: Centrifugal forces in statically balanced blades (figures are theoretical only).

This is not the case in practice, because aerodynamic forces are also acting on the rotor, as mentioned at the beginning.

4. The aerodynamic forces

The main rotor's task is to provide lift, or thrust, in order to lift the helicopter. The lift is produced by the rotor blades, which have an airfoil section similar to that of a wing. This airfoil encounters an airflow when the rotor rotates. When the blades are set with positive pitch, a greater or smaller amount of lift is produced, depending on the speed of the airflow. This lift raises the blade, and the thrust is transmitted via the blade, the blade connections and the rotor hub to the helicopter.

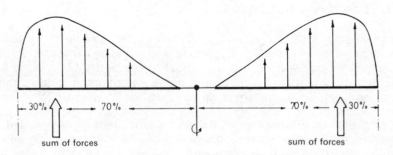

Fig. 59: Lift distribution along the rotor blades.

As fig. 59 illustrates, the lifting force on a rotor blade is not equal at all points along the blade's length. It is weak close to the hub,

68

and increases towards the tip. In theory, the lift would reach a maximum at the tip, where the speed of airflow is greatest, but this is not so. Towards the tip, the airflow breaks down into various vortices, which reduce the lift produced. If all the individual lift forces are imagined as a single force, then this force acts through a point 70% along the length of the blade, or 70% of the rotor 'span'.

The result can be imagined as a battle between two forces on the rotor blade: the centrifugal forces try to hold the rotor blade exactly horizontal (assuming the shaft to be vertical), while the aerodynamic lifting forces attempt to raise the blades, and lift them above the horizontal. The result is a certain 'dihedral' effect on the rotor blades, known as the 'coning angle'.

Fig. 60 should explain this:

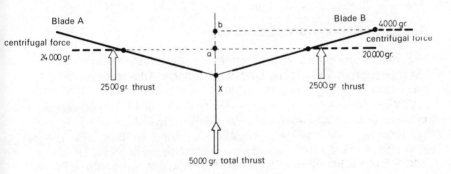

Fig. 60: Lift and centrifugal forces acting on the rotor.

The whole rotor rotates, so that lift is produced by the blades. In our example, each blade produces 2,500 g of lift. This 'thrust' raises each blade at a point about 70% along its length (exaggerated in the diagram). The centrifugal forces, shown dotted, try to pull the blades out horizontally, counteracting the lift, and a certain equilibrium is achieved: the 'coning angle'.

But: As can be seen in Fig. 60, a dynamic imbalance is now present, caused by the aerodynamic forces, if we refer to the values given in the preceding explanations.

Why?

If we consider the left-hand blade A, raised by the thrust, it can be seen that the centrifugal force (at 24,000 g) acts in one plane, which is above the rotor shaft connections. It is 'pulling' to some extent to the left through point a) on the imaginary extension of the shaft.

This is not true of blade B, which is being raised by the same amount as blade A by the thrust. There are virtually two centrifugal forces acting here: 20,000 g from the blade's weight, and 4,000 g from the ballast weight fixed to the tip for static balancing. The fact that the blade is now raised means that these two centrifugal forces are no longer acting in one plane, but in two, one above the other. 20,000 g is 'pulling' to the right at point a) on the imaginary extension of the shaft, but 4,000 g is 'pulling' significantly higher up at point b). The total is again 24,000 g, but the two forces are acting in different planes, and that means that the main rotor shaft is unequally loaded. The result is an oscillating force, and severe imbalance. The problem gets worse at higher thrust levels, with their attendant greater blade pitch, as point b) becomes further away from point a).

5. Summing up the various blade forces

a)   The position of each rotor blade is determined by two factors; one is the thrust which is trying to move the blade upwards, and the other is the centrifugal force trying to hold the blade horizontal. *These factors alone* determine the angle, 'dihedral' or coning angle of the blades. The blade holder at the rotor hub has virtually no influence; it can be fully articulated, and needs no mechanical stops.

b)   The weight of the rotor blades must be equal and distributed equally along the blade length, to ensure that the centrifugal forces are equal, as they are based on the sum of the blade weights. This will ensure that the forces act in the same plane even when the blades are raised, and that they act through the same point in the imaginary extension of the rotor shaft.

c)   The airfoil of each rotor blade must be identical, so that the lift is distributed equally along both blades. The point at which the sum of the thrust produced by each blade acts will then be an equal distance from the main rotor shaft. This ensures that the blades rise evenly and equally.

These rules must be adhered to very strictly in rotor systems with collective pitch control, in which the rotor blades produce more or less thrust at constant revolutions by altering their pitch col-

70

lectively. The blades can only produce an equal amount of thrust if the airfoils and the pitch settings are identical, and this condition will produce an even and balanced coning angle.

This point explains the relative insensitivity of a control system without collective pitch control, in which the thrust is controlled by varying the speed of the main rotor (standard control system). Here the centrifugal and lift forces vary at almost the same rate (as a function of the square of the peripheral speed), with the result that extreme aerodynamic imbalances occur much less often, and are much less powerful.

With modern helicopter models these problems can be got round by using high rotor speeds (17–1900 r.p.m.) and comparatively heavy rotor blades (150–180 gm per blade). The heavy blades rotating at high speeds produce greater forces, to the extent that the rotor will remain horizontal and no coning angle will arise. For example, a 1·4 m diameter rotor with opposed 180 gm blades turning at 1900 r.p.m. produces a force of about 250 kp per blade. (See C.G. estimates, Chapter IX. 6.)

6. Blade twisting, or torsion

The centrifugal forces which pull the rotor blades outwards in a horizontal plane (or more accurately, at right angles to the rotary axis), effectively act through a certain point along the blade length from the rotor axis (70%) as in Fig. 60, but it is also important at what point they act across the blades' chord. See Fig. 61.

If we consider the cross-section of a rotor blade airfoil, there is a centre of gravity. The weight of the blade can be imagined to act through this point. The centrifugal forces, which try to hold the blade horizontal, or try to pull the blade downward when it is moved upward, act through this point on the chord.

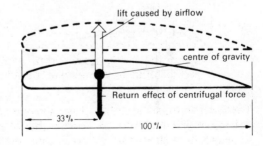

Fig. 61:
Centre of mass and centre of lift in one line. Lift caused by airflow.

At the same time the aerodynamic lift produced by the airflow is affecting the blade. The lift forces produced are distributed very differently over the airfoil, but it is again possible to imagine the lift to be acting through an imaginary point. This is known as the 'centre of lift'. It would be ideal if, as shown in Fig. 61, the blade's centre of gravity, with the downward force acting through it, and the centre of lift, with its upward force acting through it, were in the same position, and cancel each other out in a vertical line.

In fact, the situation is different, and not ideal, as shown in Fig. 62.

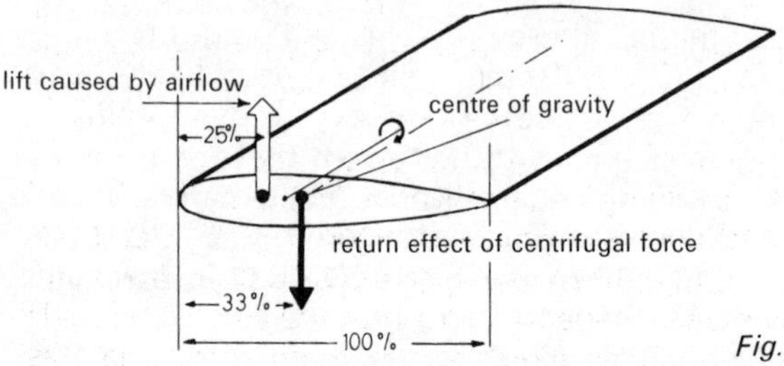

lift caused by airflow

centre of gravity

25%

return effect of centrifugal force

33%

100%

Fig. 62

Here the centrifugal force tending to return the blade acts through a point about 33% across the blade chord, while the lift acts at about the 25% chord mark. The two forces act in different directions, and the result is a twisting movement or torsion of the blade. If the blade is not sufficiently stiff to withstand these forces, the blade will suffer from flutter. During the flutter cycle, blade pitch increases, thus increasing the lift, and reinforcing the torsional effect. This 'snowballing' effect can become so powerful that the helicopter becomes completely uncontrollable.

By choosing a suitable airfoil, the designer tries to move the centre of lift as far rearward as possible, and he also tries to move the centre of gravity as close to the centre of lift as possible by concentrating the weight of the blade close to the leading edge.

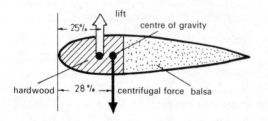

lift

25%

centre of gravity

hardwood

28%

centrifugal force balsa

Fig. 63:
Reduction of blade twisting by moving centre of gravity forward (hardwood L.E. strip, balsa T.E. strip).

This can only be achieved by adding weight to the leading edge, or at least by making the leading edge strips as heavy as possible, and the trailing edge strips as light as possible.

In Fig. 63, our example shows that the chosen airfoil's centre of lift is at 25% chord, while the method of blade construction (heavy L.E., light T.E.) has moved the centre of gravity forward to about 28% of the blade chord. Here the difference between the two points is relatively small, and the resultant torsional forces will be relatively small. In most cases they can be kept in check by correspondingly stiff rotor blades.

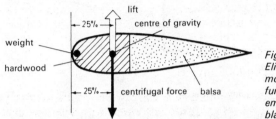

Fig. 64:
Elimination of torsion by moving the centre of gravity further forward, achieved by embedding a weight in the blade's L.E.

In Fig. 64 we have practically the ideal situation. The sum of the lift forces acts once more at the 25% chord point. By embedding an extra weight in the leading edge, the blade's centre of gravity has been moved so far forward that it is also at the 25% chord mark. In this case the two forces act through the same vertical line; it is now irrelevant how great these forces are, as in every case they will counteract each other, and will not apply torsion to the blade.

7. The effect of blade torsion on the control system

In the standard rotor design, in which the rotor blades' pitch is set by the designer, and not varied (thrust is controlled by varying rotor speed) blade torsion forces generally have little effect on control.

The blades are set at a certain pitch angle, and rigidly fixed to the rotor hub at that setting. Torsional forces are therefore directly transmitted to the hub, and do not place a load on the control components. If the blades are reasonably uniform, these forces balance each other out from blade to blade via the rigid connecting components. The only proviso is that the blades should be stiff enough, and not capable of torsion along their own length, which could lead to a tendency to flutter.

73

The situation is different with a collective pitch rotor. Here the individual blades are able to rotate to vary the pitch, and therefore do not directly support each other. All the torsional forces are transmitted directly and in full to the control pushrods.

The possible magnitude of these forces is illustrated in the example given in Fig. 65.

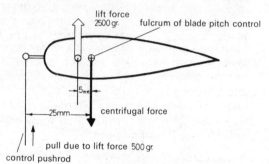

Fig. 65:
Example showing transmission of torsional forces to blade pitch arms and pushrod.

If the centre of lift is just 5mm in front of the centre of gravity, as in the previous example, and the lift produced is about 2,500 g, a 25mm long control arm will be subjected to a pull of 500 g! On a two-bladed helicopter weighing about 5000 g, and having two blades each producing 2500 g of thrust, there will be a load of 500 g on each pushrod, i.e. a total of 1000 g on the pitch control servo! This example illustrates how critical the design and matching of the rotor components are in keeping control forces to the minimum.

If the main rotor blades are not fixed exactly symmetrically, further damaging forces will result, as in Fig. 66.

In the example shown, blade A is fixed too far forward in the direction of rotation. It is extremely 'nose heavy', so that all the blade movements are transmitted strongly to the control arm a). However,

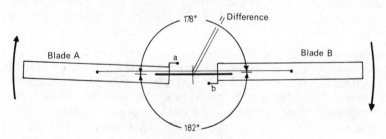

Fig. 66: Incorrect, asymmetrical mounting of rotor blades.

74

the crucial point is that the total centre of gravity of the two blades is now offset from the axis of rotation. This can be determined by drawing a line between the centres of gravity of the two blades. The line misses the axis of rotation by a certain amount, and this could lead to very severe vibration.

Today the main rotor head is equipped with forked blade connectors with only one fastening screw for the blade. The blade can also pivot on this pin and will automatically right itself so that the operating line of the blade's centre of gravity will run through this hinge.

Through suitable choice of spacing 'X' of the fastening hole in the rotor blade one can essentially influence the blade speed and control power. For the differing components such as blade airfoil, centre of gravity, pitch, rotor speed, model weight, airflow in forward flight, control power of the stabiliser, damper of the rotor etc. to have any influence, the construction of a rotor head must make many compromises in order to reach optimum power.

These compromises, and their effect on connection points, are not obvious in the finished result, but long series of tests and considerable experience have led to the end product.

If you are not 100% certain that you understand all these ramifications do not attempt to make alterations to the rotors or connections on a manufacturer's model, which leaves the factory fit to operate correctly within the makers' specifications. Even small and apparently insignificant alterations can give rise to all sorts of trouble.

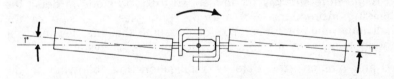

Fig. 67: Rotor blade adjustment through lead/lag hinge.

75

IV. Constructional techniques for the model helicopter

1. General

When deciding on a method of construction for a model helicopter, you must realize that a machine of this type represents a compromise solution to many individual technical problems. Hence it is often not possible to compare different model designs directly, as each design represents a self-contained unit, in which the designer's aims and philosophy play a very important part. Generally speaking, the designer is able to emphasize a particular flying characteristic by choosing a particular compromise, providing he fully understands the subject.

It is also important for the modeller to consider the fundamentals of design so that he realizes that it is not advisable to alter a particular chosen principle of construction. Usually he will only be able to change individual components, and then he risks destroying the compromise system originally chosen. This is even true of apparently insignificant details.

It is therefore strongly recommended that you study in detail the building instructions and also the principles of design of the individual manufacturers. You can assume that the designer has thought very carefully about how to optimize his system.

At the moment—the date of publication—the following model helicopters are on the market, all manufactured in Germany.

BO 105 with four-bladed rotor, by Schlüter.
Jet Ranger II by Schlüter.
Bell 222 by Graupner.
Heli-Boy by Schlüter.
Cheyenne by Schlüter.

The explanations, tips and suggestions which follow refer more or less to all the models listed above, and can be taken as a guide line for model helicopter construction. When a feature is specific to a particular model, it is usually explained in detail in the manufacturer's instructions. It would be superfluous to repeat these instructions for every individual model here. I can only recommend this: read the instructions very thoroughly and keep to them.

Consider the suggestions I make in the following section only as a general indication, and as complementary to the makers' instructions.

If you think you can improve this or that feature, then consider for a moment that the designer has probably also thought the same thing, but had to seek a compromise with other equally important factors. You should also bear the price of the product in mind; many things can be improved, but the cost usually rises, and the designer then has no choice but to make another compromise in his overall technical conception in deference to production costs.

2. The fuselage 'cell'

Usually the fuselage or 'cell' is made of hand-laminated glass-fibre reinforced polyester or epoxy resin. In these designs the 'cell' represents an important load-bearing element for the whole drive system. These mechanical units usually have to be fitted fairly precisely, and hence the fuselage has to be constructed to fine limits. This is particularly true in the fitting of the various stiffeners, bulkheads, beams etc., and also in cutting the various holes needed for air intakes and outlets, silencer exit, tank installation etc. There is usually no problem here, as the manufacturers provide full-size plans, and it is possible to measure from the plan and transfer the measurement directly to the fuselage before fitting the units in place. Always take the greatest care when transferring these dimensions.

Here is an extra tip: if you have a translucent fuselage, a powerful light can be placed behind the unit; this will enable you to check that the bulkheads are correctly positioned.

The bulkheads and beams etc. are normally installed using epoxy resin (Uhu-plus, Stabilit Express, or similar). Bear in mind that slight irregularities are inevitable in hand-laminated mouldings, and that the bulkheads and reinforcements may sometimes have to be trimmed to fit. In many cases it is a good idea to reinforce the joints with an extra strip of glass mat, overlapping the fuselage and the component being fitted (see Fig. 68).

It is also very important to avoid leaving gaps and cracks behind the bulkheads and beams where oil could build up. Helicopters usually have quite a lot of oil residue inside because of their enclosed nature, and it is a good idea to guard against the long-term effects of oil by applying several coats of resin or suitable fuel-proof paint to the wooden parts.

Fig. 68:
Gluing stiffening pieces into a G.R.P. fuselage. Particularly highly stressed joints are best strengthened by applying strips of glass cloth with resin.

Do not think that the weight of the model has not been noticeably raised by the large quantity of stickers, reinforcing materials, resin and glass mat etc. It is very easy to stick and strengthen 100 grammes too much.

In complicated designs we recommend that you start by assembling the mechanical parts to the wooden members, and then check that the whole unit fits in the fuselage. The bulkheads and other reinforcements can then be spot-glued in position. The mechanics should now be very carefully dismantled and removed, after which the stiffeners etc. can be securely glued in place, reinforced and sealed against fuel. It is always important during these installation jobs to make sure that the various mechanical drive components fit correctly and run true.

Fig. 69:
Installing the mechanical parts in a G.R.P. fuselage. One way to achieve a perfectly aligned, flat support surface is to grease the mechanical parts concerned and bed them into 'Stabilit Express' or a similar epoxy.

Here is an example: if the motor and gearbox are not assembled exactly in a straight line to each other, then the shafts will not be aligned correctly. There will be a 'kink' between the clutch and the clutch bell, and the result may be clutch damage; the clutch not only has to transmit the torque, it also has to act to some extent as a universal joint, and is bent backwards and forwards at each revolution. The same is true of the alignment of the tail rotor drive connections, of the main rotor connections, and the fitting of the main shaft bearings etc.

The fuselage design should also include an adequate number of openings for maintenance or adjustments. A completely sealed fuselage looks very nice, but it is better to provide a few holes in the first place if you want to avoid fumbling around 'in the dark' later on. This applies especially to the needle valve, the idle setting screw, the glowplug plug connector, the gearbox oil check facility, lubricating points on exposed drive components, the silencer fixing screws, tail rotor drive components etc.

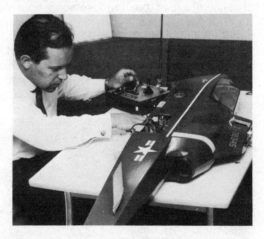

Fig. 70:
A large number of openings in the fuselage make maintenance and checking easier subsequently.

You can depend on it: if you do not make a proper job of these openings and holes in the workshop, you will have to cut them when the first little adjustment has to be carried out; and you will not be able to cut the holes cleanly then!

Another tip: the adjustor screws on the carburettor are usually rather inaccessible. Make up an extra-long screwdriver from, say, 3 mm piano wire, so that you can reach the screws through holes in the fuselage from any suitable direction.

It is also an advantage to draw in the position of the servos and the pushrods on the plan (if that has not already been done), and cut the pushrod holes etc. in the bulkheads beforehand. Generally speaking it is quite a fiddly job to drill these holes accurately when the bulkheads are already in place.

It goes without saying that all the other fittings, such as tail surfaces, control surfaces, cabin glazing etc. should be installed very carefully. When fitting a removable cabin, make sure that the fixing is really secure and cannot vibrate loose.

3. 'Open' construction

This type of design dispenses with the idea of the fuselage cell as a load-bearing component. The 'fuselage' now consists of a basic frame which may be of plastic, combined metal and plastic or wholly from light alloy. Open all-metal construction for a model helicopter was introduced with my 'Heli-Baby' in 1975 and has subsequently been continually developed.

These open structures have an unusual advantage in that in the absence of a load-bearing fuselage whole mechanical assemblies can be mounted on the basic frame, which is usually supplied as a finished structure, thus making assembly faster and, as a rule, making the model much easier to maintain and repair. Carrying out repairs on plastic structures can be difficult to almost impossible, whereas an aluminium alloy frame offers the opportunity of repeated repairs and even badly damaged areas can be cut out and replaced, using ordinary modelling tools.

Fig. 71: Typical open construction: the Schlüter 'Champion'.

Fig. 72: The same model with closed fuselage, 'Long Ranger'.

The following pages show a typical arrangement of the so-called open construction, the drawings being typical of the building instructions accompanying Schlüter models and showing all aspects in detail.

Probably the ideal is a self-supporting structure used in conjunction with a fuselage, where the framework acts as a skeleton and the fuselage is simply a skin. In this way it is possible to use different fuselages with the same mechanics and give the model an entirely different appearance. The Schlüter 'System 80', for example, gives a choice of fuselage from the BO 105, Jet Ranger, Twin Star (Ecouriee), Agusta A109, BK 117 or Long Ranger.

4. Tail surfaces

The 'tail surfaces' of a helicopter usually comprise horizontal and vertical stabilising surfaces, which become effective as forward speed increases, providing a stabilising effect around the vertical axis (yaw) and the lateral axis (pitch).

The size and position of these tail surfaces are given by the manufacturer, and they should not be altered. Modellers often make changes in this area, sometimes for no particular reason or just to improve the appearance in their eyes, and sometimes to achieve an improvement in stability.

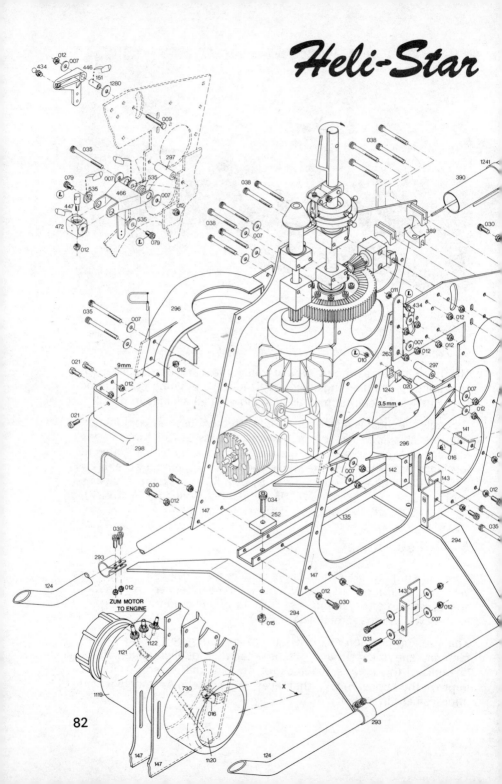

Heli-Star

ZUM MOTOR
TO ENGINE

9mm

3.5mm

82

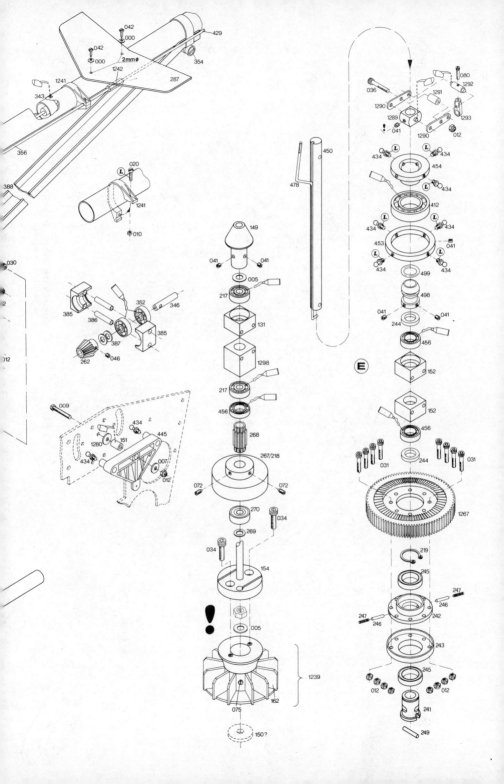

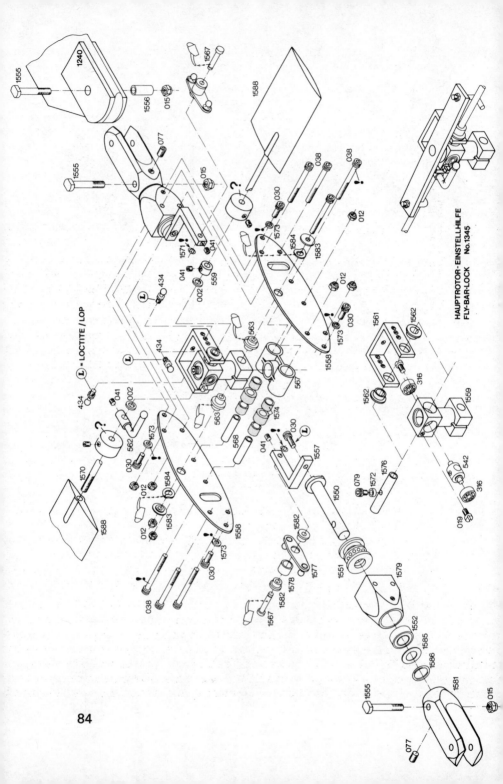

HAUPTROTOR- EINSTELLHILFE
FLY-BAR-LOCK   No.1345

L = LOCTITE / LOP

84

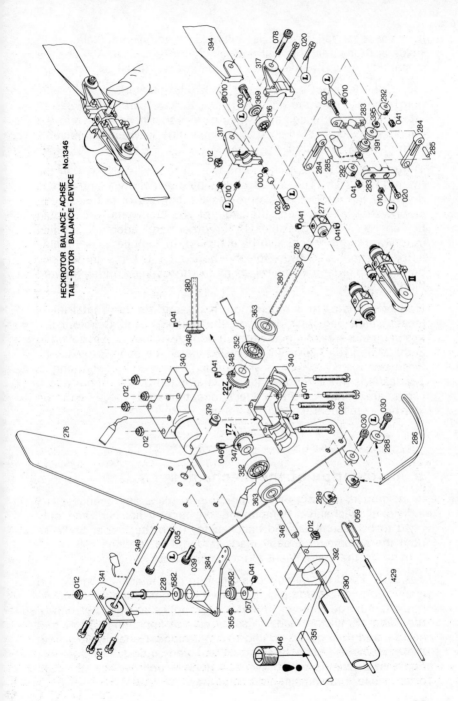

HECKROTOR BALANCE - ACHSE No.1346
TAIL - ROTOR BALANCE - DEVICE

85

If the vertical tail surface is enlarged or reduced, or altered in shape and position, this will not usually prove critical. Any change in stability around the vertical axis will not be crucial.

The same does not apply to the horizontal tail surface. Take care here! The size and the position of this surface can have a marked effect on the flight characteristics of a model helicopter, and the effects can be so marked that the machine is virtually unflyable in the forward direction!

The reason for this is that the horizontal tail is usually within the rotor downwash. The tail is struck by the airflow being forced down by the rotor, and this presses the tail end of the helicopter downward. Ideally then, the area of the horizontal tail should be kept as small as possible. On the other hand, adequate stability in forward flight should also be achieved. In such cases, a suitable airfoil section is chosen for the horizontal tail (as in full-size practice), in order to achieve maximum effectiveness during forward flight.

However, this point is much more important: the horizontal tail is located at a particular point on the fuselage, and therefore lies in a particular area of the downwash from the rotor when in hovering flight. When the helicopter moves forward, the main rotor down-wash is directed rearwards and the airflow over the tail changes. The result is that the horizontal tail is affected by an airflow which varies according to the model's direction and speed, and the 'tail-heavy moment' constantly varies.

5. Installation of the mechanics

In kit models it is not usually possible to make any changes. The individual mechanical components are factory-finished, and only need to be assembled and checked for fit in the fuselage. Please note the comments already made under 'The fuselage cell', concerning accurate alignment of the components.

Basically: Read the instructions covering mechanical assembly and installation very thoroughly. Keep to the recommendations, and do not attempt to 'improve' things. This applies to you 'old hands' too, who are all too ready to see a way of improving this or that design, and then go ahead and change things. Generally speaking, these changes 'come home to roost' very quickly, as you will find that a change which seems a definite improvement in itself, often causes problems in a different area.

I am not claiming that all the current designs are one hundred per cent technically perfect and incapable of improvement. There is always room for improvement in the technological world, and new techniques are constantly being developed, but these normally take time to come to fruition. So—keep to the sequence of construction recommended by the manufacturer, and follow the instructions regarding setting up.

It is important that you work carefully and neatly. Don't botch things. The tendency to think 'Oh, that will do . . .' is the first step to failure.

Fig. 73: Installation of R/C and servos in a 'Long Ranger'.

If something does not fit, or refuses to work, then make sure first that you have not made a mistake before you blame the maker. I am not claiming that occasional mistakes do not get past the manufacturer, but if this is the case, then he will certainly take pains to replace or modify the part concerned as fast as possible. Generally speaking, the mechanical components in the larger volume kits are made on special tools, drill jigs and similar tooling, and dimensional variations are therefore very unlikely—they occur very rarely.

A further important tip: assemble the mechanical components

correctly the first time! Install the assemblies correctly, and avoid temporary arrangements right from the start. Usually all the parts will fit correctly first time round, and what starts off as a 'dry run' ends up as the final installation. And if you forget a 'temporary measure', it will find you out. Therefore—tighten all (all!) screws right from the beginning, and install all (yes, all of them!) the mechanical components correctly. Always use the prescribed screws as supplied, and fit them in the correct locations. They must be heat-treated screws, as the loads in a helicopter can be extremely high. On no account swap hardened screws for any ordinary steel screws from your collection.

One more thing: do not overtighten screws and nuts unnecessarily. Of course, screws have to be tightened, but do not overdo this to the extent that the screw is close to failure. A screw in this condition can take little extra strain.

Where locknuts are supplied, do use them.

A drop of oil on a screw thread works wonders, and shafts, pushrods and bearings should never be installed without a drop of lubrication. Always keep an oilcan at hand when assembling, filled with a thick, heavy duty oil. On no account use thin 'sewing machine' type oil, because apart from the fact that its lubricating qualities are inadequate for the loads encountered in a helicopter, its low viscosity means that it is flung out of the bearings as soon as the parts rotate.

6. Radio control system—choice and installation

Choosing an appropriate radio system for a helicopter is not quite as easy as it may seem: opinions vary as to the necessary expense, especially with the constant flow of new and improved systems on the market, and it is hard to differentiate between the equipment that is considered good value.

This dilemma faces anyone investing in new gear, and if you are not already clear about the requirements and have no experience of radio control equipment, read everythijg in Section 7—Control Functions, first, as this will help you to see everything more clearly (or at least not be so unsure!).

Generally radio control equipment has reached a very high standard and can be expected to function over a long time with very little chance of a technical fault. To describe the various systems and brands available would take up the rest of this book.

To me the most important point seems to be that the airborne part of the equipment is not too big and as light as possible to give the model the best chance. Easy charging and maintenance of the receiver battery are also important, as is the availability of an authorised service agent for maintenance and repair. Spare servos are useful and if more than one model is flown it is better to leave servos in place and simply transfer receiver and battery. It is worth considering interchangeable transmitter modules which can store model data in the form of plug-in or built-in memory.

This last facility is quite a recent development and applies to other models besides helicopters. Plugging in or switching a memory module immediately provides the control settings, neutrals etc. previously established, which is an obvious advantage for any helicopter with multi-function capabilities and, especially, combined controls (see Section 7).

Let us first consider the installation in the model. Usually the siting of the receiver, battery and servos is predetermined and changes are difficult to make. This also applies when a gyro is fitted for tail rotor steering, but if no provision is made the gyro (not the electronic part) should always be positioned as close to the main rotor shaft as possible.

In most cases the servo positions and pushrod runs are given in the plans and instructions and it is obviously very convenient if you use the same make of equipment as is drawn on the plan.

Slight problems can arise if the designer has based his dimensions and installation on one particular system, and you are the owner of another system with different sized servos etc. You will then have to make alterations, and you should go about this with extreme caution.

The control of a helicopter is a complicated affair, and the control system must work faultlessly. For this reason you should be prepared to take great care over installing your R/C system. This is particularly true of the servos, as a neat installation, straight pushrod runs and freedom of movement are essential for faultless control subsequently; they are a prerequisite for successful flight.

There are several ways of tackling this:

Usually a 1:1 plan is supplied, with the servo pushrods also drawn in. Cut out card templates to the shape of your servos, showing the size, the position of the mounting lugs, and the position of the output arm. Move the templates around on the plan until you establish the best possible position, with pushrods accurately lining up with the output arms. Pin the templates to the plan, draw in the pushrods where necessary and decide where you will have to cut openings in the servo base plate for installing the units, plus holes for the pushrods etc.

The basic rules:

> Keep the pushrods between the servo and the mechanical component as short as possible. Keep bellcranks and levers to the minimum. Each pivot introduces a degree of backlash, and also absorbs a certain amount of power. Basically, ensure that all pushrods run straight, and are not bent.

Fig. 74: Installation of controls in Schlüter 'BK 117'.

> Bends or Z-shaped double bends result in a very soft, springy pushrod. The result is inaccuracy of control, especially when the rod concerned is under load.

When you buy a helicopter kit, check whether all the pushrods are supplied, as far as the servos, and that all the clevises etc. are included. This will make assembly much easier, and also guarantees that the servo control system will work efficiently.

The question of price also comes into this. Some manufacturers produce 'complete' kits which are by no means comprehensive. Often whole assemblies, extra pieces, conversion parts, and even the rotor blades have to be ordered (and paid for) separately. A helicopter kit should contain every single component, and in particular every pushrod and linkage as far as the servo. Then you can assume that these linkages have been tested, and have been selected as ideal for their application. You should then be sure to use them as suggested. However, if you have to select your own pushrod connections, follow these guidelines:

Quicklinks: quicklinks are relatively free-moving, but usually have a little play in the threaded end. They can only move in one plane. Metal links are especially free-moving, but they are prone to rattle about on the threaded end of the pushrod, and therefore must always be locked with a locknut. Plastic links are generally slightly stiffer in movement, but are a better fit on the pushrod and do not need locking. Snap links have proved ideal for model helicopter use. They are plastic links having a plastic pin with a small notch in the end which snaps into the other side. Long push-rods may tend to vibrate at certain motor speeds, and this can cause a quicklink to open and become disengaged. I suggest that pushrods longer than 12 cm should be fitted with short pieces of silicone tubing pushed over the links from the pushrod side to act as keepers. Be sure not to reduce the arc of movement of the link.

Ball links are ideal for helicopter work. They have virtually zero play, and are capable of movement in all directions. This feature makes angled linkages possible. They fit pushrods tightly and do not require a locknut.

One disadvantage of ball links is that they are not very free-moving; you should use a minimum of ball links in any one linkage system. In any case, before fitting a ball link, disconnect the plastic part and spread thick oil over the entire ball. The link will now move much more easily, and will be just as slop-free and secure.

One more point to watch: never screw the pushrod end so far into the shank of the plastic part of the ball link that the rod protrudes inside the cap. You risk putting a permanent strain on the link, which could eventually break.

The firm of Schlüter has now produced a new type of ball link, called a 'safety ball link', which uses a material of high dimensional stability and a special mould release technique to provide a very free-moving link. This is especially noticeable when a large number of ball links are used, as the entire linkage will remain free-moving.

These safety ball links also feature a cross hole at the end of the threaded hole, which allows you to check that the pushrod is screwed fully home.

The pushrods are usually of 2 mm diameter and are threaded M2. If your rods are not threaded, or if the length of the rods has to be altered, threaded couplers available commercially can be used. These are usually soft soldered in place, and you should take great care over this. It is just as good to glue them in place with epoxy, although you must take great care to clean up the coupler as well as the end of the rod before gluing.

The best solution technically is to obtain an M2 screwcutting die, cut the rods to the appropriate length and thread the end. Make sure that the threads are cut straight, since an angled thread produces progressive thinning of the wire which can give rise to breakage at a vulnerable spot.

If the pushrods are too long, they will have a tendency to vibrate and oscillate, as already mentioned. In such cases, it is best to add a pushrod support. It can take the form simply of a hole in a bulkhead, although the hole must be big enough to allow the pushrod free movement at all times. A hole slightly wider than the rod's diameter is usually enough to stop oscillations at an early stage.

If guide tubes are used to support long pushrods, the tubes must not be too close a fit, as dirt and oil residues will find their way into

Fig. 75: Schlüter 'BK 117' with two-blade 'Heli Star' rotor.

the tube in the course of operation and the cables will stiffen up. Plastic tubes have not proved ideal for our use, as they are never straight, and are thus bound to have a restricting effect on the rod moving inside.

The servos should always be mounted resiliently. Servo manufacturers usually supply rubber mountings, and these should always be used. However, there is no point in installing the servos with rubber grommets, only to tighten the fixing screws so hard that the rubber is completely squashed.

When mounting the servos as suggested, make sure that the push-rods are connected with the servos in line with the direction of the rod. The servo will then have adequate fore and aft support. If the servo is fitted at 90° to the pushrod, the mounting base is relatively narrow, and the servo will rock from side to side when under load. This will obviously reduce control response substantially.

Always try to use the outermost hole in the servo output arm, i.e. keep the pushrod movement as great as possible between the servo and the mechanical component. The greater the pushrod movement, the less significant will be any irregularities, and especially any slop in the linkages. When screwing a quicklink onto a pushrod, check that the rod does not project inside the link and prevent full movement. You should also check that the servo can run to its extremes of travel without jamming or being stopped mechanically. The positions for the receiver and battery are usually shown on the plan. You should bear in mind that the battery can be used to correct the model's centre of gravity, and it is therefore a good idea not to fix the position of the battery at first, to give you a choice of altering it later. The best idea here is to assemble the model completely (especially the tail components) and then establish the final position of the battery by checking the model's balance.

The battery, as the heaviest single component, should be located forward of the receiver, so that it will not damage the receiver in the event of a crash or hard landing.

Wrap the receiver in plenty of foam rubber, and secure it lightly. There is no point in using foam rubber as an insulator, only to strap the receiver down with two or three rubber bands, and compress the foam quite flat. When fitting the receiver, make sure the crystal is easily accessible.

Installation of the electronic section of a gyro unit should be similar to the receiver, especially the padded mounting; it may even be possible to mount the two together.

The mechanical part of the gyro unit is different—it needs a firm mounting with perhaps 2 mm double-sided adhesive tape. In no circumstances should the gyro rock or swing, for example if affected by a jerky main rotor. If the gyro does not work satisfactorily, check this point.

Make sure that no leads are under tension, and check that they cannot get caught up or chafe against anything. Very careful pilots go as far as to secure each plugged connection with sticky tape, to prevent the cables becoming unplugged.

The battery switch must be installed somewhere 'dry', i.e. usually on the side opposite to the carburettor and the exhaust. This will prevent the switch and the switch contacts becoming fouled up with oil. The 'on' and 'off' positions should be clearly marked. The battery lead should also be insulated from vibration. Use a small rubber band to stop any long loops of lead constantly swinging back and forth.

The aerial should be led out of the fuselage and away from the mechanics by the shortest possible route. Install a rubber grommet where the aerial leaves the fuselage, to prevent it chafing. The aerial can then be taken out at right angles to the fuselage (to the undercarriage, for example), and then led back towards the tail and tensioned with a small rubber band. In aerobatics, a loose-hanging aerial could easily find its way into the mechanics or the rotor. For aerobatic flying, the aerial must always be tensioned to the tail.

Fig. 76: Aerial looped back to the tail hoop (Alouette II).

94

7. Radio control system—control functions

Here I mean the arrangement of the control functions on the trans-mitter in relation to the servos installed in the model, and the control response of the servos.

There are widely differing views on this subject, and it is obvious that no single arrangement is the best. Opinions differ mainly because there are many model flyers who have had experience with fixed wing aircraft, and have tried to transfer their experience to the helicopter and its controls. In this respect the beginner finds it easier, as he can approach the controls without prejudice and prior influence. He will prefer the arrangement described below, which corresponds to full-size practice.

A. Basic arrangement

The motor throttle and/or pitch are controlled by the left stick. Pulling the stick back (towards the body) means: higher throttle setting or higher pitch setting, while pushing the stick forward means: lower throttle setting or reduction in blade pitch.

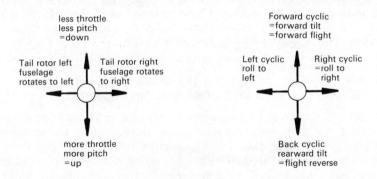

Fig. 77: Basic control arrangements on the helicopter transmitter:

The tail rotor is also controlled by the left stick. Moving the stick to the left means rotation of the fuselage around its vertical axis towards the left (nose to the left), and vice versa.

The right stick operates the swashplate alone, and therefore the direction of flight of the main rotor. Pushing the right stick forward inclines the swashplate forward; this inclines the main rotor forward, and initiates forward flight. Pulling the stick back tilts the swashplate, and hence the main rotor, backward, braking the forward movement, or initiating backward flight. Moving the stick to one side inclines the main rotor to that side, initiating flight in a lateral direction.

The right stick operates two servos (for control of the swashplate), but they can be regarded as a single function in practice, as it simply controls the direction of movement of the main rotor. It is irrelevant whether the main rotor is directed precisely to one side or forward, or in any direction between the two. In fact the pilot can forget that this movement is controlled by two servos. Bearing this in mind, it can be seen that there are only three independent functions that have to be controlled:

1. Ascent and descent of the helicopter,

2. Rotation of the helicopter around its vertical axis (fuselage heading),

3. Direction of movement of the main rotor.

This control arrangement is the one most usually flown, and it is my opinion that it is the most logical, and offers distinct advantages, at least to the beginner.

B. Different control arrangements

There are, of course, other arrangements of the controls, and some notable pilots have shown that the choice of arrangement is not crucial to success by their displays and competition results.

The basic arrangement described above is usually abandoned when the pilot has already had considerable experience in flying fixed wing models. In this case it will always be tempting to control the helicopter in a similar way to a fixed wing aircraft. This applies in particular when fixed wing and rotary wing machines are flown alternately. Here the following rules are usually followed:

Rudder control should be transferred to tail rotor control.

Aileron control should be transferred to lateral main rotor control.

Full throttle position should correspond to full throttle setting, or maximum collective pitch on the main rotor.

Idle position should correspond to idle setting, or minimum collective pitch.

Elevator control should be transferred to fore and aft main rotor control (stick back='nose up', stick forward='nose down').

If you adopt such an arrangement, bear in mind that you will have four different functions to operate independently of each other, especially if the swashplate controls are divided between two sticks, while in the basic arrangement effectively only three functions have to be controlled.

The idea that helicopters are the same whether 'real' or models is, unfortunately, not quite true. It would be nice if with 'pull' only a climb resulted, with 'left turn' only a left turn occurred, and so on. The results of many control movements seem more or less the same, which is a bit of a drawback when learning to fly. The answer is to try to overcome these 'mutual' responses, or at least to moderate them, by combining (or 'mixing') different controls.

In the early years of model helicopters, normal fixed wing radio systems were used and it was only possible to mix controls by mechanical means. Solutions to situations were evolved by trial and error and it is worth describing something of this aspect as the principles remain valid and can still be applied to simple installations where no receiver function mixer is available. Where electronic mixing is used learning to fly starts with combined controls from the outset.

Radio equipment today is so far advanced that it is possible to buy special helicopter outfits that allow many (sometimes too many!) combinations of control, all mixed electronically. This makes flying much simpler and smoother and is explained later under D. Electronic combination.

C. Combined controls

In a helicopter in which ascent and descent are controlled exclusively by varying the motor speed, i.e. by operating the motor throttle, the one stick function and servo operate the throttle. With collective pitch the blade pitch also has to be varied, i.e. the one stick and the corresponding servo control collective pitch as well as the motor throttle. These two functions have to be matched to each other in the model. The aim should be to increase the throttle setting as the blade pitch is increased, in such a way that motor speed remains constant despite the increased load on it.

Approximate values are given in the table overleaf, showing collective pitch variation on the one hand, and throttle operation on the other.

A relationship of this kind between pitch and throttle can be achieved by a differential linkage at the servo.

The pushrods are arranged to move different distances, by connecting to the servo in such a way that the throttle pushrod has a large movement over the first part of the servo throw, while the pitch

Stick setting (Pitch)	Pitch angle of the main rotor blades	Motor setting
Minimum	1°	Idle
20%	2°	30%
40%	3°	60%
60%	4°	90%
80%	5°	Full throttle
Maximum	6°	Full throttle

pushrod has a relatively small movement. In the second half of the servo throw the relationship is reversed, i.e. the throttle pushrod movement becomes smaller, while the movement of the blade pitch pushrod increases (See Fig. 78).

It is also possible to use two separate servos to control the throttle on the one hand and collective pitch on the other. The two servos are then connected to the same receiver output, i.e. they respond to the same control signal. The servo outputs can again be set up in such a way that differential control of throttle and blade pitch can be achieved.

More important than this is a linking of the tail rotor pitch relative to the main rotor pitch. The pitch angle of the main rotor is altered by adjustment of the collective pitch control and the entire load on the main rotor system changes. This in turn requires a variation in motor power output to keep height steady and an alteration of tail rotor pitch

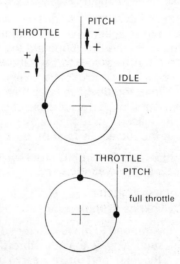

Fig. 78:
Differential linkage between throttle and pitch (collective pitch control).

98

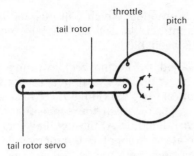

throttle

pitch

tail rotor

tail rotor servo

Fig. 79:
Tail rotor correction via trim
lever, connected to the pitch
servo.

to prevent the fuselage from turning. Precise control of the tail rotor pitch simultaneously with a change of collective pitch is required to prevent unwanted movement. Because of the moment of inertia of the fuselage small adjustments to collective pitch do not produce an immediate reaction: a delayed turn occurs if the tail rotor is not adjusted.

To this end, control of the tail rotor by its servo would be combined with a trim lever on the collective pitch (and throttle) servo, so that the tail rotor would now be controlled by both its own servo and the throttle/pitch servo. When only the tail servo is operated the tail rotor pitch setting alone alters and the fuselage will turn left or right on its vertical axis. When the throttle/pitch servo is moved to give more/less throttle and pitch, the tail rotor will also be moved proportionately. The degree of movement must be arranged so that balance is maintained between engine power, torque and tail rotor thrust, ideally keeping the fuselage pointing in the right direction.

This ideal is only rarely achieved, principally because all adjustment values are inter-related. Even small adjustments to the tail rotor, the collective pitch and anything on the engine influence the entire control system, so that if, for example, the engine needle valve is opened slightly, all other values will be thrown out.

D. Electronic combination

Combining electronic signals has the immediate advantage that all mechanical connections between individual control functions in the model are eliminated. Each control is operated by a single servo and they are directly connected before a command reaches the output gearing. As a rule five servos are used:

Servo 1 – Collective pitch
Servo 2 – Cyclic pitch (forward and rearward)
Servo 3 – Cyclic pitch (sideways, i.e. banking)
Servo 4 – Tail rotor (possibly with gyro support)
Servo 5 – Motor throttle (r.p.m.)

This servo arrangement applies to models which will operate with separate collective and cyclic controls, as well as those in which combined collective and cyclic is available.

When the collective pitch is varied by raising and lowering the swashplate and the cyclic pitch by tilting the swashplate, servos 1, 2 and 3 will operate together to control the plate (Fig. 80). To raise and lower the plate all three servos will move in the same direction, controlling the plate up and down (direction A) through bell-cranks. Servo 2 operating alone tilts the plate in direction B, but for movement in direction C servos 1 and 3 will operate in opposite directions.

This electronic combination provides, however, a single unvariable response to transmitter signals and is effectively a simpler means of interlinking servo movements than mechanical linkages. The real advantage of modern helicopter radio systems is the ability to influence in infinite ways the different control functions by, for example, signal mixing, simultaneous switching, servo interchange etc.

In this area there are virtually no limits to electronic technology and helicopter equipment can bristle with levers, knobs, adjusters and trimmers that have the benefits of reducing possible errors, though a beginner might well be overwhelmed when faced with such apparent complexity. To be absolutely clear, under ideal conditions a comprehensive transmitter and a well-tested helicopter are undoubtedly the best help to a beginner. Use of a pitch control joystick on such equipment will ensure a clean, vertical take-off with r.p.m. staying constant and no tendency for the model to turn, for example. The proviso is the 'ideal conditions': for lone hands without experience or competent assistance electronic combinations are, initially at least, not very much help, because in order to be able to set them it is necessary

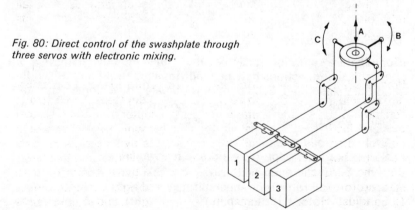

Fig. 80: Direct control of the swashplate through three servos with electronic mixing.

to fly the model, and for that it is necessary to . . . etc. There is also the point that extravagant equipment cannot really alter natural ability and owning it does not mean that you will fly any better!

In spite of all this, investment in sophisticated gear is no bad bargain. It just takes a little time, even with an experienced helper, to master it, to realise its potential and to make maximum use of what it offers.

E. Combined possibilities

As has been suggested, there are masses of combination possibilities and the following examples can only be touched on briefly. The list is by no means complete.

a) Constant motor or rotor speed.

An unloaded main rotor (zero incidence) will be sensitive to throttle control and continual operation of a conventional throttle system would be needed to maintain constant r.p.m. throughout different manoeuvres. Increasing collective pitch (and appropriate adjustment of the tail rotor, see later) increases the load on the motor. Through a pitch combination system, throttle will automatically be linked to pitch setting, i.e. as pitch is increased and rotor load rises, engine output increases correspondingly, or if the throttle is altered, pitch will automatically increase or decrease (taking into account other possible control combinations) to maintain constant speed.

b) Tail rotor balance.

The tail rotor balances torque rotation, which varies according to the main rotor loading. A 'tail rotor combined pitch' control maintains balance by automatically altering tail rotor pitch as the main rotor collective pitch is changed. More main rotor pitch requires more tail rotor pitch, but because the tail rotor power requirement differs, its pitch combination must also include linkage to the motor.

c) Tail rotor gyro.

Precise adjustment of the tail rotor for differing loads is extremely difficult and as a result gyro control has been developed. The gyro is sensitive to the slightest rotation of the helicopter around its vertical axis and feeds back a signal via the receiver which then provides a control command to the tail rotor servo. This flying aid is not only helpful to beginners but also for experts, as it will usually react faster than the pilot. Settings for the gyro include gyro sensitivity, gyro steering (often controllable separately left and right), remote setting (gyro adjustable from the transmitter during flight), and remote on/off (switching from the transmitter). There are further possibilities such as exponential setting (providing stronger control movements at the extremes of displacement or vice versa) and 'over-control' where deliberate flight movements can be made by altering the gyro.

d) Dual-rate switching.

In calm weather or delicate hovering only small control movements are likely to be required, but in rough conditions or aerobatics coarse applications may be needed. Dual-rate switching varies the response of the servo to transmitter stick movement, so that large stick movements can be switched to give large or small control responses. Sometimes one switch affects all controls but more usually each control has its own rate switch.

e) Trim switch, forward flight or hover.

Different trims may be required for forward flight and hovering (rotor tilt or bank, tail rotor) largely because of changes in airflow. A switch can change 'flight trim' to 'hovering trim' or vice versa.

f) Pitch limit setting.

A pitch switch can be used to set varying pitch limits (maximum and minimum) and examples might be normal flight $-2°$ to $+6°$, aerobatics with inverted flight $-6°$ to $+6°$, autorotation $-4°$ to $+12°$.

g) Autorotation switching.

A switch on the transmitter will cut off the motor, change the main rotor pitch to autorotation and cut out the link to the tail rotor (to stop simultaneous turning of the tail rotor).

h) Autorotation training switch.

This produces the same actions as (g) except that the motor will not be cut but reduced to a pre-set idle. The idling will be set manually in advance. The model can thus be 're-started' if the autorotation does not succeed or if after practice the flight is to continue. Usually the autorotation switch can be operated only once per flight.

i) Inverted flight switching.

Through a combined switch (sometimes separate ones) the functions of tail rotor, main rotor pitch and rotor tilt can be reversed; tail rotor left becomes tail rotor right, positive pitch will be negative and forward tilt will be back tilt. The model will thus steer exactly as in normal flight. However, it isn't quite that simple, as motor and pitch setting must also be switched to inverted flight.

102

These are the main combination functions which are customary and flying can be easier and better with them. If you think about the possible malfunctions when a single switch operates a number of quite complex actions, however, you will understand why I am a little sceptical about these multitudinous possibilities. If you are not very careful in the setting-up process you will rapidly get totally confused and end up by not flying at all. In such a case there is only one answer — go back to the beginning and start again. It happens to even the best experts!

Advice for the beginner

Start with throttle preselection and pitch combination for constant r.p.m. *(a)* but make sure that the motor is not over-revving. Then add tail rotor pitch combination *(b)* together with tail rotor gyro *(c)* with gyro sensitivity adjustment and, later, gyro direction control (adjusted at the receiver end, not on the transmitter).

Learn to fly with this array and in due course try the autorotation switch for autorotation training *(h)*, which will give you the ability to bring your model back down undamaged should the motor cut at any time.

These special transmitters also offer further facilities for reversing and mixing. A helicopter's trim in hovering flight is different from in forward flight, and transmitters are available on which you can switch from hovering trim to forward flight trim. This is no bad idea, and is particularly helpful for aerobatics.

All these reversing, trim and combination facilities are certainly a help to the expert, but their inclusion complicates the transmitter greatly, with a mass of knobs, levers, trim wheels and adjusters, and they cannot be recommended for the beginner, and only with reservations for the average flyer.

8. Motor installation

The position of the motor is usually laid down, and is determined by the manufacturer's choice and arrangement of the mechanical components. A few types of model are designed to accept one make of motor only, specifically designed for that model, and this has the advantage (especially for the designer) that the whole drive system, the motor installation and even the cooling system can be precisely matched to each other, and the installation can be specially arranged for that motor.

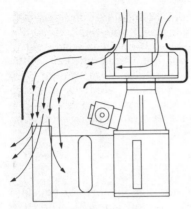

Fig. 81: Unsatisfactory cooling flow with in-correct cooling head.

Fig. 81a: Schlüter Mechaniken SHC10 helicopter motor with mounted fan and specially-designed cooling head.

The disadvantage of this type of design is that the buyer *has* to buy that motor, even if he has a suitable power plant already, or prefers a different make. Modifications to accept a different motor involve a great deal of work.

For this reason, designs in which the mechanical components form a self-contained unit are usually preferable, as they allow the buyer to fit his choice of motor.

Not every motor, of course, is suitable for helicopters, and this applies to some so-called 'helicopter motors' from several manufacturers. Often the crankshaft end on which the fan, clutch, etc. are mounted is so rough, untrue or mis-shapen that it is impossible to get the impeller to run quietly. The inaccuracy often results from modification of the crankshaft end of a motor meant for a propeller. Similarly, right-angled air cooling ducts are frequently thoughtlessly mounted on 'helicopter motors' with no regard for the fact that they may not be suitable for certain types of engine. This especially applies where narrow-spaced shallow fins or square fins are used.

On the latter case the ducted air striking the flat side of the cylinder rebounds; it will only cool the centre of the cylinder a little and the underside barely at all. A motor with deep and widely-spaced circular finning is far better for ducted air cooling, and naturally the ideal is one which is supplied with the flywheel/fan ready fitted.

Fitting different makes of motor and connecting them to the mechanics is usually no great problem, although the mounting dimensions
of the motors concerned do vary. Motor installation has to be left
variable, which means that there is scope here for the model builder
to make mistakes.

For this reason, please note the following: The motor must always be
perfectly aligned to the mechanical components with which it is
connected. The parts actually fixed to the motor, such as the flywheel,
the fan, the clutch etc. must be fitted accurately, and checked very
carefully.

For reaching the carburettor adjustor screws, I recommend that you
drill holes where necessary and make up a special extra-long screwdriver for carrying out these adjustments, as mentioned under
'The fuselage cell'. You will be glad you made the effort!

The fitting of a silencer is usually provided for in the design,
and only slight alterations are possible. Note that the exhaust
radiates an amazing amount of heat, and therefore also requires
a certain amount of cooling. It is a good idea to ensure that the
exhaust is either located in the airflow, or is fanned by part of the

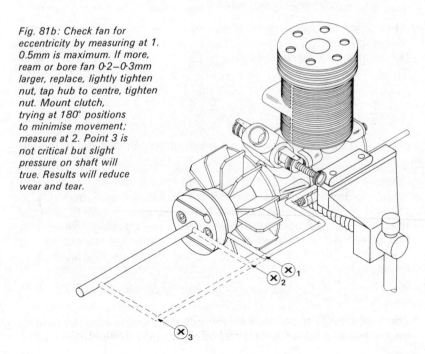

Fig. 81b: Check fan for
eccentricity by measuring at 1.
0.5mm is maximum. If more,
ream or bore fan 0·2–0·3mm
larger, replace, lightly tighten
nut, tap hub to centre, tighten
nut. Mount clutch,
trying at 180° positions
to minimise movement;
measure at 2. Point 3 is
not critical but slight
pressure on shaft will
true. Results will reduce
wear and tear.

RCHM–D*

rotor's downwash. If the silencer is not a good fit on the motor's exhaust stub, a small amount of epoxy resin or silicone bath sealant can be used to form a gas-tight seal.

The choice of a suitable plug for the motor generally depends on the fuel used as well as the make of motor, and the motor manufacturer usually recommends a type. R/C type plugs, with idle bar, have proved excellent.

9. Tank installation

The position of the fuel tank is usually laid down in the instructions, or at least suggested, and it is normally advisable to follow the designer's recommendations. You should assume that the most effective tank position has been found and tested under all conditions during prototype testing. You have to bear in mind, of course, that sometimes the best possible location for the tank is not available for design reasons, and a degree of compromise is unavoidable.

Basically, however, the following rules apply to tank installation:

Fit the tank at the same level as the carburettor if at all possible, so that the changing fuel level does not have too marked an effect. Locate the tank as close as possible to the centre of gravity (close to the main rotor shaft), so that the changing weight of fuel does not cause too great a shift in the model's centre of gravity, although in practice a distance of up to 20 cm from the main rotor shaft in the longitudinal direction causes no great problems. The varying weight of fuel can easily be compensated for by the transmitter trims. This does depend to a large extent on the size of the model.

The feed pipe from the tank to the motor should be very carefully laid out in the fuselage, and protected from kinks and chafing by rubber grommets if necessary. Take particular care over fitting the end of the fuel tubing onto the nipples, as it is easy to damage the material. Use only the best quality fuel tubing. Never use fine-nosed pliers for this job when the nipple is inaccessible, as it is hard to avoid making a hole in the tubing by this method. It is better to remove the tank, the cooling shroud, the exhaust or something else in order to fit the tubing using your fingers and great care.

The feed pipe from the tank to the motor should not be too narrow gauge (small I.D.—at least 2 mm I.D.), so that the fuel flow is not obstructed unnecessarily. All tanks need *ventilating,* so that air can reach the tank to replace the fuel leaving it. Keep the tubes clean, as a blocked ventilator will stop the flow of fuel. Many a motor has stopped in flight because the ventilator was partially or completely blocked, and not because the tank connections were faulty! For example, a drop of thick oil residue is enough to block the tank air vent, and fuel flow is reduced to the point at which the motor runs lean and stops!

It is usually best to provide a third tank pipe for filling, so that no tubes need to be disconnected. It is a very good idea to take the filler and air vent tubes to suitable nipples mounted directly on the fuselage side. This allows all fuel tubing to be arranged inside permanently, and the tank can be filled at any time without having to open up the model, or even stop the engine. Here too, great care must be taken to ensure that the air vent is kept free of dirt, and of oil residues in particular.

Clean fuel, clean fuel containers, and clean filling equipment are absolute necessities for an undisturbed flow of fuel to the motor. Filler tubes dangling in the dirt are an abomination. They must be sealed off with a plug. But here again, have care: if that plug has been floating around in your toolbox, it is probably far from clean.

To be entirely safe, always keep filling until a little jet of fuel sprays out of the vent tube, so that any dirt in the tubes is not forced into the tank. In the same way, the filler nozzle should be checked for cleanliness before filling. If you follow these rules, motor failure due to fuel problems should not occur. Even a filter will be superfluous, because quite apart from the fact that the filter itself can become blocked, it is better to make sure that no dirt enters the tank, rather than filter it out at the last moment just before it reaches the motor.

10. The rotor head

A model helicopter's rotor head is without doubt one of its most important components, as it determines the basic flying character-istics, and to a large extent also the effective flight performance. Opinions differ on the most suitable design of rotor head for a model helicopter, and they vary from the highly complex (and therefore highly priced) to the simple, robust designs suited to day-to-day flying.

There is a basic division of opinion concerning control of vertical movement: rotor speed control, and collective pitch control. In

Fig. 82: Graupner 'Bell Twin Jet' rotor head with one-piece stabiliser bar and collective pitch control through the hollow main rotor shaft.

the first case the control of thrust and therefore vertical movement is achieved solely by altering the motor's throttle setting, and therefore the speed of rotation of the main rotor. In the second, the aim is to maintain main rotor rotational speed as nearly constant as possible, while controlling vertical movement by altering the angle of incidence of both blades at once (collective pitch control). The pros and cons of these systems have already been explained (see II 10 and II 11).

The control of horizontal flight direction, both in the fore and aft and lateral directions, is achieved nowadays without exception by cyclic pitch control. All the systems developed so far are based to a greater or lesser extent on the Hiller system—a stabiliser bar with control paddles. In principle, these systems are the same as the one I used in my first flights in 1969 and early 1970, and which has proved to be the most suitable for model applications. Little has changed in the principle, but modern differences are:

1. The swashplate acts only on the stabiliser bar which carries the paddles. The main rotor blades then have cyclic control from the stabiliser bar. This is the Hiller system.

2. In addition to the Hiller control, the main rotor can also be

controlled direct from the swashplate, similar in effect to the Bell system. This is referred to as 'Bell-Hiller Control' or 'Bell-Hiller Mix'.

The Hiller system, entirely indirect in operation, has the distinct advantage that small control forces are sufficient to operate the stabiliser bar with its paddles. This protects the servos, as the forces required to control the main rotor blades are produced by the paddles alone. The drawback of this method is that a degree of delay between the control input and the reaction of the main rotor always has to be accepted. This delay can be reduced to a minimum, by making the paddles relatively large (powerful aerodynamic reaction), and at the same time relatively light (low inertia when reset by the control system).

In the second system, there is an unusually rapid reaction by the main rotor system, as a certain amount of the cyclic pitch variation

Fig. 83: Kavan 'Jet Ranger' main rotor head. 'Bell' control system with divided and non-controllable stabilising bar like the Bell system. Collective pitch controlled by raising and lowering swashplate. Paddles make system flyable, adding stability though not controllable. (Kavan, 1972.)

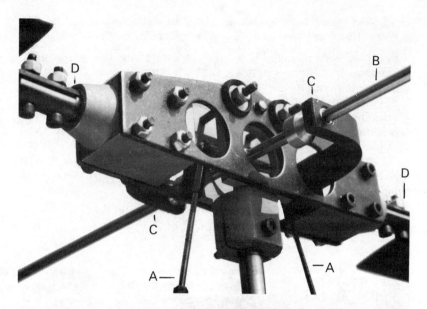

Fig. 84: The Schlüter 'Expert' main rotor head for the 'Bell Huey Cobra', 'D-S 22' and 'Gazelle'. Raising the swashplate raises both pushrods A. This raises the stabiliser bar B. The two blade pitch control arms C are thereby lifted, and the pitch of blade holders D is collectively altered. By tilting the swashplate, the two pushrods A move in opposite directions, thereby rotating the stabiliser bar B and effecting cyclic pitch control of the control paddles (not shown in the picture) on the ends of the flybar.

(depending on the ratio used) affects the main rotor blades immediately, and this means that the delays inherent in the Hiller system are eliminated. This type of rotor is intended for the expert, because it demands relatively fast reactions on the part of the pilot, and also requires a corresponding degree of understanding of the technical aspects, as well as a high degree of care in setting up and balancing the rotor blades.

Although developed for the more experienced, many beginners like the Bell-Hiller system. It requires a great deal of concentration because of its fast reactions, but on the other hand right or wrong control movements are instantly obvious. Stability can be increased by weighting the ends of the stabiliser bar without affecting the fast response and while it is possible to see which control has been given the model will not make large changes of position or attitude immediately.

The Bell-Hiller system is now the most frequently employed and

Fig. 85:
'Standard' rotor head without collective pitch. The swashplate only controls the stabilising bar and paddles; tilting the bar tilts the seesaw. Blades have constant angle and flapping hinge. Climb and descent by change of rotation speed. (Schlüter, 1973.)

Fig. 85a: Main rotor head for aerobatics from the Schlüter System '80', utilising a mixture of the Bell and Hiller systems. Here the mixing levers are fitted on the blade pitch lever. The pushrod running downward effects direct control from the swashplate, while the pushrod running upward from the mixing lever superimposes the stabilisation of the stabiliser bar. Collective pitch from pushrod in split rotor shaft (emerges on right in photo). (Schlüter, 1977.)

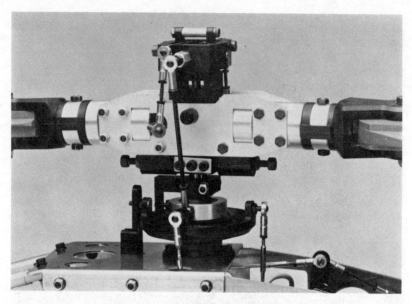

Fig. 85b: Direct control without stabiliser bar. Collective pitch controlled through hollow main shaft, cyclic pitch from swashplate. Both movements combine in head and act directly on blades. (Graupner, 1979.)

Fig. 85c: 'Heli Baby' rotor head with collective pitch through pushrod in slotted rotor shaft. Pushrod moves over swashplate in sliding housing, controlling pitch in place of stabiliser bar of the Hiller system. Swashplate controls only the stabiliser bars. (Schlüter, 1975.)

112

practically all manufacturers use it. Apart from small differences in positioning and materials for the pushrods, stabilising bar etc. the only real variation is in the operation of the collective pitch control. Two systems have proved most successful:

1. Combined pitch control through the swashplate. Here the swashplate controls not only cyclic blade pitch (by tilting) but, by moving vertically up and down, the collective pitch. Swashplate rising=more collective pitch and vice versa.

2. Separate pitch control. The swashplate takes care only of cyclic pitch, collective pitch being controlled by a separate rod sliding in a groove in the rotor shaft or sometimes inside a hollow shaft.

Both systems have been well proved and which is used depends usually on the design of the rotor head or how the Bell and Hiller elements are combined. Details can be seen in the photographed examples.

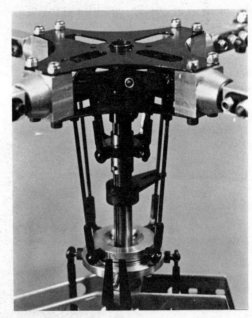

III. 87b:
Four-bladed rotor head of the Schlüter System '80 'BO 105'. The blades are directly controlled, collective and cyclic pitch controls are mixed in the rotor head, and the blades have individual blade fixings with flapping hinges.

Rotors can sometimes be seen without stabilising devices, in which case they are controlled direct, dispensing with stabiliser bars, paddles and other Bell-Hiller appurtenances. The rotor heads are extremely simple and are considerably more streamlined, much more like a full-size helicopter in fact.

Direct blade control was introduced at the end of the '70s, but has not

Fig. 86:
'Superior' all-metal rotor head for expert and duration flying. Bell/Hiller combination, double blade positions with axial setting, ball bearing stabiliser bar.

found a widespread following. Flying with this system demands 100% concentration and the pilot cannot take his eyes off the model. The rotor reacts with marked directness, one might say furiously, and the model must be flown precisely the whole time. Flight with a stabiliser bar is on the whole much pleasanter, although this only applies to two-blade rotors. With a growing desire to build three- and four-blade rotors, direct control might catch on further.

Improvements in control techniques and, particularly, more advanced radio equipment have made direct control slightly less formidable, but extremely high flying ability is still required of the pilot.

Fig. 86a: 'Champion' rotor head, also all-metal but lighter though strong. Common stabiliser bar beneath blades allows direct control and Bell/Hiller mix. Blades are axially secured to a flexible mount with twin ball-races.

114

Rotor heads of model helicopters also differ in the methods by which they are attached to the main rotor shaft or the rotor mast. The different types are: a fully articulated suspension, a system with flapping hinges, and a system with a more or less rigid suspension.

Fully articulated rotor head suspensions usually excel in smoothness of running and stability in hovering flight, although there is a disadvantage in that the pilot cannot always see the reaction of the fuselage to a control input intended to redirect the main rotor in the horizontal plane. This feature is improved by incorporating individual flapping hinges, and in the case of 'rigid' rotors, with a greater or lesser degree of damping built in, the fuselage responds to a main rotor movement immediately. The last-named rotor types do have the disadvantage that they transmit any inaccuracies in blade tracking to the whole helicopter system in the form of fairly severe vibration. These rotor types depend to a very great extent on very precise balancing and setting up of the rotor blades.

The individual makes differ from each other to a greater or lesser extent, and should be considered as self-contained units—and each one is a compromise. It is therefore superfluous to go into the technical details of each design; I can only repeat my strong recommendation that you keep to the building instructions given by the manufacturer, and observe them fastidiously. This applies to the rotor head in particular, as the considerable centrifugal forces of the rotor blades produce unusually high forces in this area. Particular care is called for in this phase of construction.

The golden rule here must be—do not make *any* changes to *any* components, and in particular to the blade fixings, the screws, and the prescribed spacing of the screws.

Special care is also called for in balancing the stabiliser components, and in particular the stabiliser bar and paddles. Even very minor errors in adjustment will be very noticeable later on, and control problems can often be traced back to improper assembly or incorrect adjustment of the rotor head.

Once again, an oilcan filled with heavy duty oil should be at hand during assembly of the rotor head parts, and during later maintenance work. Make sure that all pushrods, bellcranks, bushes etc. are absolutely free-moving, and I recommend that any ball links used should be dismantled, oiled, and reassembled to ensure freedom of movement.

When linking up the control pushrods—for collective pitch, or even just for cyclic pitch control—be sure that they are as per the in-

Fig. 87: Four-blade rotor with direct control. The aluminium blade housings are ball-bearing mounted with axial pinning and flexible-mount flapping hinges. The housing unit is screwed to the rotor hub.

Fig. 87a: Different blade housing units with varying numbers of rotor blades can be mounted on the rotor head hub provided the correct positioning of screws is allowed for. This three-blade rotor is on the same hub as the four-blader above.

structions, and perfectly straight. Safety is the main priority here too, and no experiments or alterations of any kind should be undertaken.

11. Rotor blade construction

Virtually all rotor blade designs in models today make use of wood, which has proved an ideal material for blades as it is torsionally stiff, possesses excellent tensile strength and is easy to work with modelling tools.

Rotor blades are of composite construction, using timbers of varying strengths and densities. The aim is to use the strongest and hardest woods for the leading part of the blade and relatively light material for the rest. A typical example is a rotor blade with the forward one-third made of shaped beech and the rear two-thirds of balsa. Very successful blades have been made by lamination, and again the forward part of the blade has made use of heavy, hard timber and the aft part some lighter wood.

For direct control of the rotor head without a stabiliser bar, the rotor blades need to be very heavy to provide the necessary stability. Some makers (e.g. Graupner, Kavan) will cut small pockets in the blade tips in which lead weights can be glued. This works extremely well but there is a chance of the weights breaking loose and flying off like bullets if the rotor hits the ground while spinning.

With this in mind Schlüter blades for direct control incorporate a steel rod about 3 mm dia. bonded into a groove along the blade leading edge, the root end of the rod being bent round the blade and bonded securely in place. This not only increases blade weight but moves the blade C.G. forward. Naturally, the blades can be ruined in a crash, but the steel rods will remain attached to the rotor hub and cannot fly off. This form of construction has now been patented.

The F.A.I. Sporting Code actually forbids the use of metal in rotor blades for competition flying, at least for new models. The rules undoubtedly exist for safety reasons and are promulgated by the official international organisation. It is not, however, the metal which is dangerous, but how it is used. A lead weight of 20–30 gms glued in a blade tip could certainly become a projectile if a blade was demolished, but if lead powder is poured into a suitable recess (without glue) in the event of an accident the ballast weight would scatter safely in the air. I use a non-springy wire rod and in the case of a rotor write-off it will not fly off – it tends to wind itself around the rotor head.

117

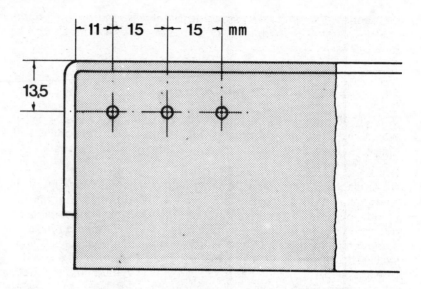

Fig. 87b: Weighted rotor blade from the Schlüter System '80', using an embedded rod to increase weight and move the C of G forward.

In order to get round the metal ban, resourceful modellers have discovered a so-called bronze powder which is not detectable by a metal detector. This adds weight and also makes the blades tougher.

Blade weight is another important subject. Normally the weight will be determined by the materials and method of construction used by the manufacturer, who will have made exhaustive tests on its airfoil section, attachment, damping, C.G., centre of lift etc. etc. as well as on the mechanical strength of the rotor head itself. If you therefore fly a model with the blades supplied, or authentic replacements, no problems should arise and blade weight will be correct.

There are, however, always fliers who will want to uprate the performance of their models and the major factor is likely to be autorotation. For autorotation the blades cannot really be too heavy; since any kinetic energy produced makes starting autorotation quicker, i.e. on the power being shut off the heavy rotor will remain spinning faster than a light one, which decelerates quickly. However, the heavier the blade and the faster it turns the greater the forces produced, so that more power is needed in the controls, perhaps especially for blade pitch. Here there are limits and the builder has to accept a compromise.

Fig. 88: Rotor blade mounting. Note single pivot screw and reinforcement.

An answer is the use of glass-reinforced plastic (glass fibre) rotor blades, which are sold separately and are nicely made, reliable components. They have, however, a whole lot of other characteristics which may not compare with the original blades and may therefore require considerable modification before use.

The effect of blade weight on thrust (lift) can be seen in the three sample estimates in Section VII 6; look it up now! Example 2 shows the effect of adding a 30 gm weight to the blade tip.

Blade loading is quite considerable and for this reason the area of attachment to the rotor head requires particular attention. Hardwood reinforcement is customary at the root and the actual blade fastening will be a single 4 mm dia. screw passed through a stub of tube secured in the blade. The tube length and screw tightness should be such that the blade is held firmly in position with enough friction to prevent it moving easily. It will automatically set itself in the correct position by the forces generated when the rotor is revolving.

It will be obvious that the position of this pivot bolt is of considerable importance, primarily in respect of its distance from the blade leading edge, and it will, perhaps less obviously, have an effect on rotation speed and control efficiency. The distance from the c.g. depends on blade cross-sectional weight distribution and blade width (usually 55–65 mm) and will have been established by test bench experiments in the normal course of events.

Naturally the blade section chosen and blade size, i.e. blade width and rotor diameter, are also crucial factors in rotor and hence flying performance.

Speed-controlled rotors using the popular Clark Y section, with its flat bottom and cambered top surface, have almost completely disappeared. Today's preference is almost exclusively for double-convex, symmetrical sections where both surfaces are curved. Sections such as NACA 0012 and other fully symmetrical aerofoils familiar to modellers are the most popular.

x %	y %	x %	y %
0	0	30	6,00
1,25	1,89	40	5,80
2,5	2,61	50	5,29
5,0	3,55	60	4,56
7,5	4,20	70	3,66
10	4,68	80	2,62
15	5,34	90	1,45
20	5,74	95	0,81
25	5,94	100	0.12

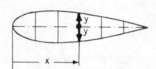

Fig. 89:
Airfoil coordinates for the NACA 0012.

These symmetrical sections are usually preferred for use with collective pitch. The reason for this is that the centre of pressure travel mentioned above (shifting of the centre of lift) is exceptionally low, and that the control forces required, once set up correctly, remain relatively constant, and consequently provide a non-varying load on the control system at different pitch settings.

The fully symmetrical blade also has a somewhat better lift to drag ratio than the CLARK Y sectioned rotor blade. All this assumes that the blade airfoil is really precisely maintained.

The 'disadvantage' of the symmetrical airfoil is that it is somewhat more difficult to construct because it has no flat undersurface, and is therefore difficult to check for alignment. You cannot get by without special checking and setting jigs with these sections.

An essential ingredient of all efficient rotor blade sections is first class workmanship of the rotor blade itself, a clean and sharp trailing edge, and uniformly precise and smooth surfaces. In particular, the blade's trailing edge is of great importance. Manufacturing methods cannot usually provide the desired sharp trailing edge, and the modeller then has to finish the blades off himself.

Fig. 90: Covering a rotor blade with self-adhesive film.
A. Remove backing paper, and lay the film on a flat surface, adhesive side up.

Fig. 91:
B. Place what is to be the top surface of the rotor blade on the film, leaving a strip 1 cm wide at the trailing edge.

121

Fig. 92:
C. Pull the film round the trailing edge (keeping the edge sharp) and fix down onto the uncovered side of the blade.

Fig. 93:
D. Pull the rest of the film round the leading edge, pull taut and press down onto the rotor blade.

122

Fig. 94:
E. Press film down very firmly overall, and check that there are no bubbles trapped, especially at the leading and trailing edges.

The normal method of obtaining smooth surfaces is to cover them with a suitable self-adhesive covering film (see Figs. 90–94).

A rotor blade can also be covered with very thin self-adhesive aluminium foil. Schlüter kits include such foil, which has the effect of producing almost an airfoil-sectioned aluminium tube. It is not, however, the easiest material to apply. The blade must be absolutely straight and sanded to a very smooth surface and the foil must be smooth and perfect; it tends to roll up as the backing paper is removed, which will spoil it for the job. You are quite likely to have to make a second attempt. If it is laid on smoothly without stretching (it is only 0.2 mm thick) the result is an exceptionally stiff blade, well worth the effort.

12. Balancing the rotor blades

It is obvious that it would be relatively difficult, and therefore expensive, for the manufacturer to produce rotor blades which are ideal in every respect. Quite apart from the extra work required on the surfaces, there is the important task of balancing the blades.

Even in the full-size helicopter world, where the rotor blades are constructed under strictly controlled and highly precise conditions,

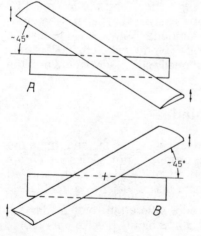

Fig. 95:
Centre of gravity positions
along the blade length and
across the chord.

each blade has to be individually trimmed at the final stage.

In view of the variety of blade designs, and the static, dynamic and aerodynamic forces acting on a rotor blade, the balancing of the model helicopter's rotor blades assumes great importance.

The rotor blades (Fig. 95) should meet the following requirements:

a) Identical total weight

b) Identical longitudinal centre of gravity (X)

c) Identical lateral centre of gravity (Y)

d) Identical blade section and surfaces.

a) The total weight of the rotor blades can usually be found very simply by using suitable scales. Kitchen scales are not ideal, however, as their graduations are much too coarse. Letter scales or a similar precision balance are preferable, as they are usually able to show up a difference of a few grams.

b) The blade's centre of gravity, and therefore the distance X along the blade's length can also be found easily. Clamp a blunt-edged knife in a vice, with the blade's edge exactly horizontal,

Fig. 96:
Establishing the blade's centre of gravity by balancing the blade at an angle on a sharp edge, then repeating the process. For details see text.

124

and projecting above the vice jaws. Now place the finished, covered rotor blade on the knife blade, and shift it to and fro until it balances. Press the rotor blade gently down onto the knife blade, so that a slight impression is left on the rotor blade's under-surface.

c) The lateral centre of gravity, given by distance Y, is found in a similar way, but with the blade laid at 45° to the knife blade. Make an impression as above, then move the blade through 90° and repeat (see Fig. 96).

Where these two impressions cross is the centre of gravity, and dimension Y can be measured. Both blades of the rotor system are balanced in this way, and you can check that they match each other. With a 3 bladed rotor, all three blades have to be balanced, with a 4 bladed rotor, all four, etc.

There may be any of the following differences between the blades:

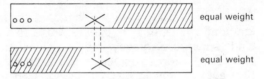

Fig. 97:
Rotor blades of equal weight, but different centres of gravity.

As shown in Fig. 97, the total weight of the two rotor blades may be identical, but the centres of gravity may be in different positions. Remedy: The blades are given an extra layer of covering film in the shaded areas, until the centres of gravity coincide. You have to be careful that the total weight remains identical, i.e. apply the same amount of film to each blade, and at the same distance from the centre of gravity X.

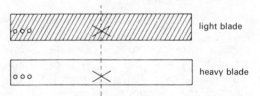

Fig. 98:
Centre of gravity the same for both blades, but one blade lighter than the other.

In Fig. 98 the centre of gravity of both blades is in the same place, but one blade is lighter than the other. Remedy: the lighter blade is given an extra layer of covering film over the shaded area, until it reaches the same total weight as the heavier blade. Take care here only to apply film over the entire length of the blade, so that the centre of gravity X does not move.

125

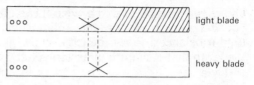

Fig. 99:
Blades of different weight and different centre of gravity.

light blade

heavy blade

In Fig. 99 we have two blades whose total weight and centres of gravity are different. Remedy: Apply extra covering film to the shaded area of the lighter blade, until the total weights are identical. If the centres of gravity are still different, apply film equally to both blades as in Fig. 97 until the centres of gravity coincide.

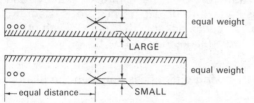

equal weight

LARGE

equal weight

equal distance — SMALL

Fig. 100:
Both blades equal weight and same longitudinal centre of gravity, but distance of centre of gravity from L.E. very different.

The blades shown in Fig. 100 are of the same total weight, and their longitudinal centres of gravity are also coincident, but the one blade's centre of gravity is much closer to the leading edge than the other blade's. Remedy: The blade with the more rearward centre of gravity is given an extra layer of film over the whole length of the leading edge, shown shaded. The blade with the more forward centre of gravity receives an equal amount of extra film, applied along the length of the trailing edge.

Other combinations of imbalance can easily be remedied by combining the solutions given above. In all cases you must recheck the blade's centre of gravity and total weight when you have adjusted the balance. The more precise these adjustments, the better will be the blade tracking.

It goes without saying that the balancing exercises described above demand considerable care, and it has been shown in practice that a modern rotor system can tolerate various imperfections without completely destroying its flying capability, provided that it is not overstressed by a demanding pilot. On the other hand it should be stressed that accurate balancing of the rotor blades provides refinement of rotor control, contributes greatly to smoothness and stability of flight, and not least reduces the wear and tear on the servos and other control components.

The excellent performances of top pilots are due in no small part to fastidious balancing of the rotor blades, and accurate setting up of the whole rotor head and control system.

126

13. The simple method of balancing

The processes just described are aimed at achieving absolutely perfect balance of the rotor blades, and at helping you to recognize possible errors which can be traced back to incorrect construction. Thank goodness, this sort of effort is not absolutely essential in normal practice, and simpler methods of balancing are usually satisfactory. Here we are assuming that you have a pair of straight rotor blades of, as far as possible, equal weight. This is not always the case with wooden blades. The following method is then adequate for ordinary day-to-day flying.

After very carefully balancing the flybar and the other rotor head parts, the rotor blades are attached to the rotor head. They are fixed in place at right angles to the flybar, and in a perfectly straight line to each other, and adjusted correctly using the manufacturer's adjusting gauge.

As a rule, one rotor blade will prove to be heavier than the other, and if the rotor is fully articulated this will be obvious at once, as the heavier blade will tip downward. With a semi-rigid or even a rigid rotor, the rotor head has to be removed from the model, and its flybar placed on two supports. The heavier blade will now tip down.

You now take a piece of covering film, brightly coloured if possible, and remove the backing paper. Stick the film onto the lighter

Fig. 101: Typical method of balancing a main rotor. The main rotor blades are corrected by adding film until the blades hang level – using a ruler to measure the height.

127

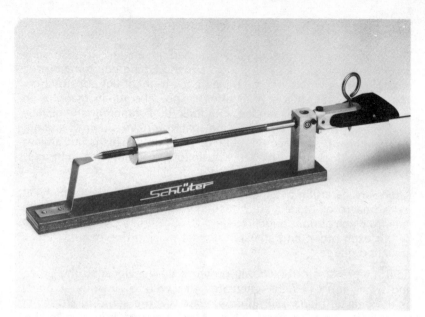

Fig. 102: The Schlüter blade balance is simple and accurate to use.

blade temporarily. Begin at the rotor tip and work towards the rotor hub, depending on the weight of film required. You will very quickly find out how much extra film is needed to compensate for the heavier blade and keep the whole rotor system horizontal. When the correct area of film has been determined, the film is carefully applied to the existing covering. Do not use small patches of film, as they will soon come off; always use strips long enough to go right round the blade and overlap. You can be sure that these pieces will not get blown off, even after a long period of use.

Always use a different colour on each blade tip, as this makes adjustment of blade tracking easier.

If the main rotor runs out of true in spite of careful balancing, the following additional check should be carried out:

Using a Schlüter balance, place a finished blade in the mounting and screw the balance weight along its rod until the pointer aligns with the zero bracket, which gives very sensitive setting. Find the heaviest blade and use the setting for this to bring the other blade(s) to weight by adding foil or film. The balance is suitable for all current conventional rotor blades of 14 mm thickness (at the mounting) with 4 mm pivot screws.

Fig. 103: Tail rotor hub on the 'Heli-Star' model.

14. The tail rotor

All the model helicopters currently on the market utilize a tail rotor with collective pitch control, i.e. the tail rotor blades can be adjusted in pitch by a servo. This makes it possible to control the thrust of the tail rotor independently of its rotational speed.

The tail rotor is generally driven by a drive shaft running right to the tail, with a 90° bevel gear drive, although a system using a thin, flat belt and pulleys has also proved suitable.

An important factor in the efficient operation of the tail rotor is absolute freedom of movement, and lack of play. This is another area where the manufacturer's instructions should be strictly adhered to, and I would also suggest applying a drop of oil to all the tail rotor joints from time to time.

Tail rotor blades are nowadays supplied as finished plastic mouldings, and may be fully symmetric or biconvex asymmetric in section. Use only the blades recommended by the manufacturer.

When fitting the tail rotor blades, bear in mind that they should be able to fold back in case they strike the ground, thus avoiding damaging the blades and the drive mechanism. Of course, they

129

should not be fixed so loosely that they flap about. If this were so, it would be difficult to control their pitch accurately.

The degree of pitch of the tail rotor is generally given by the manufacturer, and depends on the basic design, the type of tail rotor section, the tail rotor rotational speed, tail rotor diameter, and the blanking effect of any vertical tail surface. There are no general rules here. The tail rotor setting for hovering flight is usually about 4—8 degrees, and varies between about 10—12 degrees at one extreme to about 0—+2 degrees at the other.

Special care should also be taken over the tail skid, which should be carefully and securely mounted, so that the tail rotor has maximum protection in the event of a hard landing.

15. Landing gear

With few exceptions, the landing gear consists of normal aluminium tube skids with cross pieces usually made of aluminium section. Sometimes the cross pieces are of wood. The landing skids, and especially the cross pieces, should be made of a material which will deform under the shock of a hard landing, without breaking. The great advantage of this arrangement is that the model will stay upright even after a hard 'arrival', even though the skids may be badly bent. This protects not only the fuselage, but also the main rotor.

For initial training, extra wide-based landing skids are recommended.

Fig. 104:
'Landing gear' of the 'Bell Huey Cobra'. The struts running upwards on the sides were mounted on powerful compression springs, and could absorb the shock of very hard landings.

They provide a relatively widely-spaced support, and make it possible to survive skewed landings undamaged. Another alternative is the use of floats, which are also ideal for learning to fly over water.

16. The finish

There is not much to say on this subject, as a model's finish really depends on the builder's skill, and whether he wants a pure flying machine or a particularly nice-looking one. The wooden parts are treated in the usual way by applying several coats of sanding sealer, sanding between coats. Only fuel-proof paints should be used. Glass-fibre reinforced plastic fuselages should be rubbed down all over with fine glasspaper to provide a better key for the paint, and small irregularities or pinholes can usually be filled with filler paste. There is really no limit to the amount of trim striping, lettering, logos and other self-adhesive embellishments that can be applied. The same is true of fitting out the cockpit or cabin. Do bear in mind, however, that it is easy to add a lot of weight in this way.

One more thing seems very important to me:

It is normally very difficult to be sure of a helicopter's attitude at all times, as there is no wing for a reference point. When a helicopter is flying sideways at some distance, the silhouette also disappears, and at times this leads to incorrect control inputs by the pilot. For this reason I would recommend that the model's nose be painted a bright colour to contrast with the model's tail. Vivid, fluorescent colours are ideal.

V. Accessories

1. General

There are certain standard accessories needed for operating a model aircraft and the same applies to model helicopters. These items make it possible to carry out the essential checking and maintenance jobs in an efficient manner. You really ought to make a point of assembling a toolbox specifically for this purpose, and equip it and look after it. Generally speaking, it does not make sense, financially or otherwise, to buy one set of tools for workshop use, and another for flying field maintenance. If you find the toolbox a permanent position in the workshop, and make a point of returning any tool to it after use, you can be sure that you will be in a position to carry out any job at the flying field. You will probably make up this or that special little tool, and you will have certain alignment gauges and setting-up aids, a certain type of fuel, glowplugs etc. If these are stored in the toolbox from the start, you just have to pick up the toolbox and you are fully equipped.

It may seem strange to mention this sort of thing here, if it all seems normal and obvious to you. However, I have often seen modellers arrive with a beautifully built and fully-equipped model, and then they have not been equipped to change the plug, because they have left the spanner at home! Not to mention any specific checking or adjusting jobs. Anyone who can afford model flying, and model helicopters in particular, should have a few pounds left for a proper set of tools for the flying field. To some extent your success depends on this.

2. Adjustment for main and tail rotors

Adjustment gauges are either provided by the kit manufacturer, or at least instructions are given for making them. Some sort of gauge is essential, to make it possible to check and correct the pitch angle of the main rotor blades and tail rotor blades. Do take them to the flying field, as you will need to carry out field checks on occasion.

132

Fig. 105:
*Schlüter universal
adjustable angle gauge.*

There is a Schlüter accessory for this purpose in the form of a universal adjustable angle gauge. It is suitable for all rotor blades currently available and precise measurement and adjustment from $-20°$ to $+20°$ can simply be carried out.

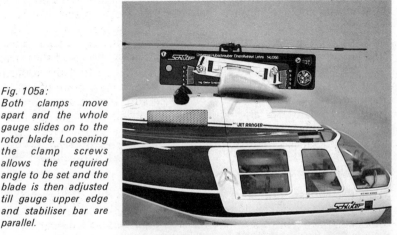

Fig. 105a:
*Both clamps move
apart and the whole
gauge slides on to the
rotor blade. Loosening
the clamp screws
allows the required
angle to be set and the
blade is then adjusted
till gauge upper edge
and stabiliser bar are
parallel.*

Fig. 105b:
*Adjusting tail rotor.
Gauge clamped to fin,
main scale at zero. Cor-
rector scale set to
required angle and
butted to rotor bearing.
Adjustment from $-10°$
to $+10°$ possible.*

Fig. 105c:
Specially made
ball pliers allow
easy dismantling
of ball and socket
universals from all
mechanisms.

3. Starter and starter battery

When choosing an electric starter for a model helicopter, bear in mind that not all the available makes of starter are equally suitable for all models.

Primarily adequate power providing a good torque to the model's starter connection is required. A rubber cone on the starter engaging a

Fig. 105d:
Gauge clamp for
stabiliser bars
locks bars while
blade adjustments
are made. Also
useful for clamp-
ing the bar against
movement while
driving to the field.

spinner or cone on the engine crankshaft extension is generally used; plug-in starter extensions allow the starter to be used from above without damaging the swashplate or rotor head etc.

Another important point in the use of electric starters is the use of an adequate gauge of cable. If you use 1–2 m of cable which is about 1.5 mm² cross section, the voltage drop when the starter is on load will be so great that only 4–6 V. will be available at the starter when using a 12 V. battery. Obviously the starter will not be able to spin the motor. Always use cable of 4 mm² cross section, and also keep the connecting leads as short as possible.

Sealed batteries are ideal for our use, as they can be operated in any position. This type of battery can be placed right by the model,

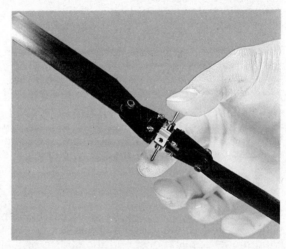

Fig. 105e:
Another simple Schlüter accessory is a 5 mm dia. pivot rod held between finger and thumb for balancing tail rotors, where good balance is essential to avoid vibration.

keeping the leads as short as 20–30 cm. This will guarantee the full battery voltage at the starter. Sealed batteries also have the great advantage that they cannot cause damage through acid spillage during transport. Ordinary lead/acid batteries are just as suitable, but the risk of acid spillage is extremely high, and after a short period in the toolbox or car boot, the items close by the battery will usually show signs of attack.

It must be said that sealed batteries are not entirely uncritical in their charging requirements, as overcharging will rapidly ruin them. It is worth buying an automatic charger for these units, and although the whole system is not cheap, it will pay for itself in the long run. Returning from a day's flying, you connect up the battery to the automatic charger and forget it until the next flying day.

4. Glowplug battery and glow clip

No special helicopter units are needed here. A normal, commercially available rechargeable plug battery of 1.5–2 V. is adequate, with the usual connecting lead and glowplug clip. A suitable charger is also needed, of course, although ordinary 1.5 V. dry cells can also be used. If you do not overload these cells, one will last a whole season.

In some helicopter designs it is difficult to gain access to the glowplug, and in such cases a remote plug connector is the solution. Various versions are available in model shops. The plug is connected to a fixed lead which ends in a socket mounted on the fuselage skin. The battery is then simply plugged into the socket for starting.

5. Tools

The main points about tools have already been mentioned. If you cannot take your complete workshop tool kit with you, as I have recommended, you must at least be sure to take allen keys of 1.5, 2 and 3 mm sizes, and box spanners of 5.5 and 7 mm, plus a plug spanner which suits your type of helicopter. Don't forget any special screwdrivers for the idle screw etc. Additional items are the usual assortment of pliers, screwdrivers and spanners, as well as the adjustment gauges mentioned earlier.

6. Fuel

Opinions on the right fuel for a model helicopter vary extremely widely. An all-round 'best' fuel has not even been found for fixed wing model applications, and the choice of fuel certainly depends on the type of motor, the motor settings, the choice of glowplug, the type of application, and even the climatic conditions at the time.

There is nothing against using nitrated fuels, and there is no disputing that they have been used successfully for many thousands of flying hours. Nevertheless, I personally do not use this type of fuel, preferring normal 'straight', non-nitro fuels. I usually keep to an 80:20 methanol/lubricant mixture, although the proportion of lubricant can be reduced to 17–18% depending on the type used.

It is my opinion that straight fuels are best for model helicopter use, as the process of combustion takes place more gently and evenly. This means an equally gentle and regular power output to the mechanical parts, and thus the whole drive and transmission system is subjected to less strain.

I have carried out many experiments using high-nitro fuels on my own test stand, and the results have shown that these fuels tend to cause fairly severe and spontaneous pre-ignition; the result is certainly a degree of extra power, but on the other hand the power delivery is extremely rough and jerky.

You have to bear in mind here that the modern single cylinder two-stroke internal combustion engine, as used in model aircraft and helicopters, is a very unsuitable type of power plant. At most one third of each revolution actually produces power. Roughly another third produces a braking effect due to compression, i.e. the motor's speed slows down substantially. The final third of each revolution encompasses scavenging, gas exchange etc, and the transition between acceleration in the combustion phase, and deceleration during the compression phase, takes place in this third.

Therefore if a general increase in power is achieved by using a special fuel (or glowplug, or engine setting, or course), the power increase can only manifest itself in this one third of the motor's cycle. This means that at 12,000 R.P.M. the entire drive system receives 12,000 propulsive shocks every minute, which are transmitted through the whole chain, placing very heavy loads on all components. These loads increase as the flywheel mass of the motor is reduced, i.e. as the damping of the combustion impulses transmitted to the mechanics is reduced.

For my part I prefer an addition of about 3% ordinary five star petrol to the fuel. I have successfully used this mixture for years in fixed wing aircraft, and use virtually nothing else in my helicopter flying. The result is more even and flexible combustion, and it seems somewhat cooler running.

7. Other matters

I strongly recommend that you take a few pairs of crystals with you to the flying field, so that you can change to a less popular or unused frequency. This is particularly useful when you arrive at the flying field with a new helicopter. You can let other flyers carry on flying, while you find a quiet corner with your vacant frequency, and carry out your preparations in peace and quiet.

It is usually essential to take along a few important replacement parts; these would include at least one set of main and tail rotor blades, various other screws, locknuts etc., and perhaps some main rotor components, like the flybar, control levers, main rotor shaft, blade holders etc. A roll of red adhesive tape is also a good idea for marking points to be remedied.

RCHM–E*

VI. A day's flying

The following procedures apply to the beginner and the experienced or expert flyer alike. The only difference lies in the fact that the experienced model helicopter flyer will have learned that certain basic rules have to be adhered to under all circumstances, if he is to start a day's flying competently and bring it to a successful conclusion, without any damage, if possible! Many things will already be a matter of routine, and scarcely need thinking about, as they are absolutely second nature. The beginner, however, ought to know the details of these procedures.

1. Final checks

Let's start from the assumption that you have carefully constructed your model, following the manufacturer's instructions, and think you are ready to go. Nevertheless, before setting off for the flying field, you should check over your model once more in detail.

By 'check over' I do not mean simply glancing at a few screws, pushrods or other components; I mean assuring yourself that *every* moving part is functioning correctly.

A final check of this type would run as follows:

Check over the motor installation, and in particular check that all the motor fixing bolts are correctly fitted and tight.

Check that the silencer and silencer stub mount and adaptor, if any, are fitted correctly, and tighten if necessary.

Check that the fuel tank is installed in the correct position, and is securely held.

Check that none of the fuel lines is kinked, that they are fitted correctly, and are in the correct position.

Check that the tank's filler and vent pipes are clean.

Check all pushrods, for all four functions, for ease of movement, working from the servos to the mechanics.

Operate all controls to their extremes of travel, and check that pushrods etc. cannot jam or rub against any part.

Check that all pushrod connections are fitted correctly, and that the pins are fully engaged.

Check all ball links for freedom of movement. If necessary, unsnap the plastic part and apply a drop of oil to the ball.

Check the entire tail rotor system. Disconnect the tail rotor pushrod and check its operation by hand. Check over all retaining screws on the tail rotor, including the blade retaining screws etc.

Fig. 106: Another form of 'final check'.

Check over the main rotor. This includes all rotor blade fixing screws, all the fixing screws of the complete mechanical system, including locknuts etc., and the correct fitting of all control pushrods, control arms etc. Bear in mind the high centrifugal force of the rotor blades, and take particular care over this area!

Check the rotor blade pitch settings. Check the fixed setting of non-collective rotors, and check the minimum and maximum settings of collective rotors.

Are all the rotor blade tips of different colours, to aid blade tracking checks?

Check that the entire drive system is securely mounted, rotates freely, and the gears are meshed correctly. Oil the mechanics, or check the oil levels in the gearbox, topping up if necessary.

Is the starter belt in place?

Are all the batteries fully charged?

Are all the other R/C system components properly fixed, and isolated from vibration by foam rubber?

Is the aerial correctly deployed, and not coiled up in the fuselage?

Is the machine's centre of gravity still in the correct position, or has it shifted as a result of adding detail fittings or a pilot in the cabin?

Fig. 107:
Checking the centre of gravity.

This list probably covers the most important items, although by no means every single point which the pilot has to consider before a flight. You could continue the list to suit your own machine, perhaps like this:

Is the undercarriage properly fixed? Are the cabin latches in working order? Are all the fixed tail parts correctly secured, and not likely to break off? etc.

2. Preparing the accessories

Another point not to be neglected before driving off to the flying site is the preparation of the essential accessories.

The fuel is the first consideration. As is well-known, successful helicopter flying depends to a very great extent on the reliable operation of the motor, and hence on the use of a clean, suitable fuel. For this reason, always check that you have an adequate supply of clean fuel of the right type before you go flying. Having a good supply is important, in that you cannot usually find the correct carburettor settings to suit a particular fuel without carrying out several tests. Nothing is more annoying than to have to change to a different fuel after a short time, thus risking that all the carburettor settings will need adjusting again. This is especially inconvenient at flying displays or competitions, as you usually have no time for protracted adjustments in these situations.

You will also need to get the following items ready:

Electric starter with fully charged battery. Check that the connecting leads are in good condition.

Rechargeable or dry battery for the glowplug, plus connecting cable and plug clip.

Adjustment gauge for main and tail rotor.

An adequate supply of tools, cleaning rags etc.

And something else to check: Do you have adequate insurance cover for any consequence of owning and operating a radio controlled model?

3. The journey to the flying field

At first thought you might think that the trip to the flying site has virtually nothing to do with the actual mechanics of helicopters. However, if you think about it, this matter *is* relevant in some ways.

After carrying out all those detail checks on the model before setting off for the flying field, it is senseless to ruin them all by being thoughtless or careless when loading the model into the car. So check, when placing your valuable helicopter in the car, that it cannot slide about and strike anything, and will not get broken if you are forced into sharp evasive action or heavy braking. This also applies to the accessories, such as replacement parts, tools and toolbox, fuel container, starter battery etc. All these items will stay on the floor of the boot under normal driving, but are transformed into missiles if the car brakes suddenly, completely destroying your valuable cargo. For the same reason, the parcel shelf in front of the rear screen is no place for these items.

Depending on the size of your car and the helicopter, it may be necessary to dismantle some components for transport. If so, please mark the pushrods to be disconnected, and also the correct position of the main rotor, for example, so that you can reassemble the model exactly as you set it up and checked it in the workshop.

When loading, always check that the rotor blades do not get caught up, or obstructed by other luggage. You risk thwarting all the careful rotor adjustments you have made. Make sure that the tail rotor cannot be knocked out of adjustment.

If it is possible to leave the main and tail rotor blades on the helicopter in transit, it is a good idea to use a rubber band to stop these parts waving about as the car moves, at least on longish trips.

If there is still some fuel in the tank, please remember that the inside of a car can become very warm, and the air in the tank can push the fuel out of the tank. Make sure the tank is ventilated to prevent this occurring. It is most important to disconnect the fuel supply to the motor, otherwise the motor may be completely flooded when you arrive at the flying field.

Do disconnect the starter supply leads. Otherwise you may find that the starter switch is knocked 'on' as it moves around, and the starter will run riot inside your toolbox!

It is also advisable to disconnect or otherwise secure the plug lead from the battery. On one occasion my toolbox began smoking terribly because a tool had short-circuited the contacts of the plug clip.

4. Ready for action

When you have arrived at the flying site, refit any parts removed for transport, and check their settings. Check once more that nothing has suffered any kind of damage in transit.

Fill the fuel tank. Always bear in mind the great commandment: Cleanliness, cleanliness, and yet more cleanliness! Are the filler tubes dirty? Squirt a few drops of fuel into a rag, so that any dirt in the fuel line will be washed out, and not reach the tank. Check that the tank is adequately vented, or the pressure in the tank will rise, pumping fuel to the motor and hopelessly flooding it. If the fuel tank is above the level of the carburettor, it is best to disconnect the fuel line to the carburettor or shut it off with a clip.

Connect up the glow plug lead to the battery, and check that it is working by connecting a spare plug.

Get out the electric starter and connect up to the battery. Now check that it spins in the correct direction. Otherwise this may happen to you, as it did to me once: I despairingly tried to find out why my motor would not start, and only after removing the plug, the carburettor, the needle valve etc. several times did I realize that I had just connected up the starter in reverse, and had been trying to make the motor run backwards. . . . .

Now check that your radio system is working perfectly. Wait a moment: Before switching on, check that your frequency is clear. Ask your flying friends specifically what colours they are using, and always heed the frequency regulation procedures in force at your flying site.

5. Starting the motor

After checking again that your frequency is clear, switch your transmitter on. Now switch the receiver on and check all four functions again. Set the motor at full throttle.

If you disconnected the fuel supply line, reconnect it now and open the needle valve the correct number of turns for full throttle. Usually this is about four full turns.

If the fuel tank is slightly higher than the carburettor, the fuel should now slowly flow down to the carburettor. Now start the motor without delay, to avoid your motor becoming flooded. If the

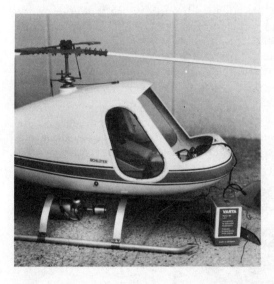

Fig. 108:
Starting procedure using a V belt: the electric starter is engaged on the belt, and the belt is pulled tight by pushing the starter downwards. Do be sure to check the direction of rotation of the starter!

tank is at the same level as the carburettor, or slightly lower, use the fingers of one hand to seal the filler and vent tubes of the tank, and squeeze the fuel tank gently so that gentle pressure forces fuel to the motor. Now reset the throttle to idle.

If your motor is belt-started, engage the starter on the belt, after checking once more that it is turning in the right direction. Hold the rotor to stop it turning, or let one blade rest against your shoulder. An assistant is useful for this task, but if he is new to it, make it clear to him that the motor will start very suddenly and powerfully, otherwise he will let go of the rotor in sheer terror.

If you are now ready, attach the glowclip and check that you have made proper contact with the plug. Here a check lamp in the circuit to show whether the plug is glowing is very useful.

Check again that the motor is set either at idle or slightly above.

Switch on the electric starter and start up the motor. Normally the motor will start very quickly, although a new motor will sometimes take longer, and may stop once it is running.

When using an electric starter, take care not to hold back the motor with the starter once the motor has actually fired, as this will prevent it reaching running speed. This applies in particular to starters with gear reduction. This type of starter is not ideal for belt starting, as the motor's speed is held right down by the starter's gearbox. In any case, try to disconnect the starter slowly after the motor has started, so that your motor can run up to speed.

At this stage you can safely advance the throttle so that your motor speeds up, but make sure the rotor is firmly held. On no account maintain this high speed for long, however, or the centrifugal clutch will be overstressed. The clutch will begin to heat up after about half a minute, and you then risk damaging the clutch.

Models with a starter cone projecting upwards are fairly easy to start, as the starter is simply pressed down onto the cone. You should take care not to damage any parts of the rotor head, however; some starters have a large head which gets in the way. Extensions are available commercially to enable the actual starter to be held above the rotor head.

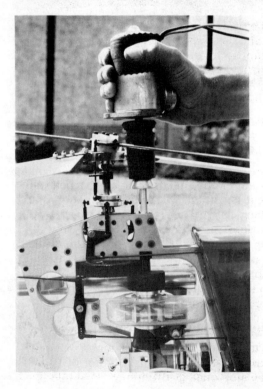

Fig. 109
Starting the motor in a Schlüter 'Heli-Boy', using an electric starter from above.

Fig. 110:
Checking motor settings at
high R.P.M. with the clutch
engaged. Take care! Do not
put the model down until
the rotor blades have come
to rest.

You can either start your motor on the ground, on a table, or on a suitable starting cradle. In this last case you can keep below the helicopter and allow the rotor to rotate above your head after the motor has started. This will unload the clutch and the other drive components, and you will be able to advance the throttle more and remove the glow clip, but with extreme caution.

When advancing the throttle for the first time, take great care that the rotor does not speed up too much, or your model may suddenly lift off. This is especially true if you are a beginner.

If your model is mounted in a training stand, on a table, or you are able to hold the model over your head with absolute confidence and safety, then you should check the full throttle performance and setting of the motor. To do this, advance the throttle slowly and smoothly, and ensure that your motor increases speed smoothly without stuttering, right up to maximum revolutions. Adjust the needle valve for maximum performance by screwing in the needle valve—you left it on the rich side for starting. As a rule, the motor's speed and main rotor speed will rise at a fairly constant rate, and the motor will run more smoothly and evenly. Continue screwing in the needle until the motor speed starts to fall off. This drop in speed generally occurs very suddenly, and it is then necessary to open up the needle again very quickly to prevent the motor stopping. The needle should now be opened again until motor speed drops slightly. This usually represents the best carburettor setting, although motors vary slightly. They are usually set to suit a particular pilot, or a special fuel, or the motor installation system, or the fuel tank position.

This does not apply to a brand new motor.

6. Running in the motor

If you have installed a brand new, un-run-in motor, you obviously cannot set the motor to full throttle immediately. The essential thing here is to run in the motor slowly and carefully.

Experience has shown that it is not essential to run in a modern, ringed piston motor on a test stand before using it in a helicopter. The motor can quite happily have its first runs in the helicopter itself. In principle this is also effective for the so-called ABC motors, although these are generally harder to start and need a longer warming up time.

It is important here that the motor is adequately and carefully cooled. You should also ensure that motor speed does not exceed 50% of maximum, and should be constantly altered. In addition the carburettor should be set as rich as possible, so that the motor is very well lubricated throughout, especially in the first few minutes of running.

Of course, the motor will not be capable of a good idle setting, so it will be difficult to keep the clutch disengaged. For this reason it is advisable to allow the rotor to spin shortly after starting the motor, and you then have the chance to try short test hops with the model.

On no account set the motor to its maximum setting straight away and even if you have the experience, do not carry out a few circuits immediately. You must take into account that during this stage the motor will change speed a lot and will lose power, sometimes even stopping dead. Some motors, especially ABC types, may need several hours before then are run in, but usually after half an hour or so speed begins to settle down and a reasonably accurate idling setting can be established.

If, on the other hand, you have the opportunity of running in the motor on a test bench remote from the helicopter, there is nothing against doing so. On the contrary, you have the advantage that your motor will have some running behind it before it is fitted into the helicopter, and that a more precise idle setting is possible. This

Fig. 111: 'Running in' the motor. Short hovering flights with the motor set very rich, with cooling off periods between flights, are a very good procedure.

also takes much of the strain off the clutch. Do bear in mind that the carburettor will require quite different settings from those needed on the test stand, when using a normal propeller.

7. Rotor checking, blade tracking

As soon as you allow the main rotor to rotate in this initial stage, it is very likely that it will spin smoothly, provided that it has been balanced properly. If this is not so, and the model vibrates severely, then some setting has certainly altered in transit. Check once again whether your main rotor is correctly balanced, and whether any settings have been knocked out of true.

These checks *cannot* be carried out on the helicopter itself, as there is always some wind to falsify the results. It is best to remove the main rotor and check it inside the car where the air is still. Shut all the doors and windows, and keep the heater fan switched off!

If the rotor runs smoothly and is well-balanced, without any severe vibration, you can proceed to check blade tracking.
Correct blade tracking means that the rotor blades are spinning in the same plane, i.e. one blade does not run higher than the other. Here is where the differential colouring of the rotor tips is a great help. The rotor is allowed to spin at a moderate speed, and you then

observe the blades from one side. You will see the blade tips clearly, and will be able to pick out by its colour which blade is tracking higher than the other. Ideally, both blades will track in precisely the same plane. Caution! Keep at a safe distance when sighting tracking.

With collective pitch control, the rotor blades are adjusted by altering the length of the blade connection pushrods. With non-collective rotor heads, the pitch is altered by undoing the fixing screws, and rotating the blade, or by slightly bending the metal blade holder. With a non-collective rotor, it is important that a large amount of thrust is produced when the main rotor is at its absolute full throttle setting, but on the other hand the model must not climb too strongly, or the rotor speed will have to be decreased by too much to initiate a descent. It is therefore best to reduce the pitch of the higher blade when altering the tracking of a non-collective rotor, if there appears to be an excess of power. This will reduce total thrust. If power seems to be inadequate, the pitch of the lower blade should be increased. Some practical experience is necessary if these adjustments are to be carried out precisely. The degree of precision is also a matter for the individual pilot.

Tracking should be checked not only at moderate speed, but also at higher and maximum revolutions. Note that the rotor blades are bound to alter slightly in pitch according to rotor speed, owing to the very large centrifugal forces, and therefore blade tracking

Fig. 112:
Checking blade tracking. In the example shown the light-coloured blade is running higher than the blade with black tape on its tip. Take care! Never get too close to the rotor. Tracking can generally be checked better from a distance of several metres.

will vary according to rotor speed. Here you can be satisfied with a sensible average value; tracking is adjusted adequately when the blade tips are not more than 5 mm apart. There is no doubt, however, that careful adjustment of blade tracking is of crucial importance for the subsequent smooth running of the whole model, and also for really precise control; so it is well worth aiming at a tracking difference of zero between the two blades.

Now check that the tail rotor operates correctly, using a training stand if possible, where the model cannot get out of control. Check that none of the pushrods is rattling against the model or vibrating severely. Is the aerial free, and not wrapped around some mechanical component?

8. Final checks before take-off

You must not expect the control settings to be 'spot on' at the first take-off; the model will not be immediately controllable even by a fairly experienced pilot. Usually a few corrections will have to be made to the trims after the first take-off. For this reason, the first attempt must not be made close to the toolbox, but at a good, safe distance from it and other spectators, even other model flyers. Take care also that your attempts do not disturb your flying friends' activities by coming too close to them. No model flyer likes it when a helicopter suddenly takes off behind or close by him. Quite apart from the fact that the whirling rotor blades represent danger, a helicopter rotor throws dirt, cleaning rags, scraps of paper etc. into the air, and it does no good to your own tools, let alone the tools and models of your colleagues, to be covered with dirt.

Before you make that first flight, carry out a last check, which you ought to commit to memory permanently:

Is there enough fuel in the tank?

Is the transmitter aerial fully extended?

Is the receiver aerial fully deployed?

Lateral swashplate control working?

Fore and aft swashplate control working?

Tail rotor control working?

Motor throttle and collective pitch control working?

Is anybody standing too close for safety?

Is the take-off area free?

Are any other models likely to take off or land?

If all is well, you are ready to go.

9. Take-off, flight and landing

If you are an absolute beginner, you can miss out the next section and go straight on to the chapter headed 'Initial training'. On the other hand, even as a beginner you will find it interesting to know how that first circuit is made, so it is not a bad idea for you to read the brief description which follows. The account of the post-flight checks is equally important to you.

Here we go:

Advance the throttle and collective pitch setting slowly until the machine lifts off. Use the tail rotor to hold the heading steady, and trim the swashplate controls to keep the model hovering about 50 cm to 1 m above the take-off point.

Tilt the nose downward, pick up speed, hold the direction steady with the tail rotor, and advance the throttle slightly. Control the rate of acceleration by altering the forward tilt, keep a check on the rate of ascent once forward speed has built up, and aim to fly the machine in a straight line by correcting with the swash-plate and the tail rotor.

Fly a left turn by applying left cyclic, and help the turn by adding a little left tail rotor. While flying the turn, apply a little back cyclic to counteract the loss of height. When the turn is complete, apply opposite cyclic to revert to straight flight. Correct forward speed with forward cyclic, and maintain altitude by varying motor speed or collective pitch setting, holding the model on a straight course with tail rotor.

Fly the second turn, downwind this time, just as before. Fly the model upwind at a moderate speed for a landing approach.

Landing approach: reduce rotor speed by reducing the throttle setting, or reduce thrust by lowering collective pitch. At the same time be sure to maintain forward speed. Hold your course straight with cyclic and particularly the tail rotor. Take great care to maintain a steady speed, neither accelerating, nor slowing down to a hover. Holding this attitude, allow the model to descend as gradually as possible, and slowly pull the nose up to decrease forward speed. When the model is close to the ground, slowly advance the throttle or increase collective pitch, to make the model flare out. Watch the tail rotor carefully at this stage, to avoid the tail coming round and making the landing cross-wind. Try to fly as accurately as possible, and aim at reducing the sinking speed until at about

Fig. 113: A 'function check' on a training stand is also useful for the expert.

50 cm altitude forward speed and sinking speed drop to zero, exactly above the intended landing spot.

Landing: with the model hovering at about 50 cm altitude, hold it completely stabilised over the spot, and allow it to descend gently onto the skids by reducing rotor speed or collective pitch slowly, all the while correcting the pitch and yaw attitudes. After touchdown, reduce throttle to idle, and let the rotor slow down and stop of its own accord.

That's it! In itself a simple enough matter—always assuming you know how to do it. . . . .

10. Post-flight checks

After landing, please clear the landing area immediately. When you are experienced and absolutely confident, you can hover back to the edge of the landing strip.

Cut off the fuel supply to the carburettor so that your motor does not flood. Switch off the receiver and then the transmitter, hand the transmitter back to the transmitter compound and return the frequency

151

peg. Bear in mind that other flyers will be wanting to use the frequency you have been using.

The next thing is to make the following post-flight check:

As soon as possible seal off all open fuel lines, especially the tank filler nipple, so that dirt cannot get into the system.

As the oil-soaked sardine is not a pretty sight, it is a good idea to clean off the dirty oil residue from your model, but be careful not to bend the pushrods, or alter any settings.

The main purpose of this clean-up, however, is to check that all of the mechanical parts are still in order. Check in particular that pushrods and other metal parts do not show signs of rubbing etc. A black smear of aluminium is a sure indication that parts are loose. Check that the exhaust is still secure, the skids have not come loose, no screws have come undone etc.

If everything is in order, and no damage has been found, protect your correctly set rotor and park your model where it is out of the way of that dangerous breed—the curious.

Make a point of remembering where the transmitter trim levers are set, and mark their positions with a pencil if possible. This is especially important if you fly other models with the same transmitter, which require different trim settings. Remember also the needle valve setting which has proved best.

Here is a little tip: I always note down needle settings using a clock face: 3.20 means 'needle open $3\frac{1}{3}$ turns'; 4.15 means 'needle $4\frac{1}{4}$ turns open' etc.

If, when cleaning and checking over your model after the flight, you turn up some little defect, it is important either to remedy the problem immediately, or at least to make a note of it.

People are generally very forgetful, and I would advise using a piece of red tape to mark any damaged area or possible source of trouble. I always keep a roll of red adhesive tape in the toolbox for this purpose.

It is best to make a rule for yourself: when something is giving trouble, or is damaged, *never* say to yourself 'it will be okay for one more flight' and carry on flying. Apart from the fact that this is dangerous and irresponsible, it is also condemning your model to an early fate, and wasting all that effort in producing it. A model helicopter is a very complex machine, and a relatively innocuous defect can be enough for a disaster.

11. The journey home

It really does seem superfluous to say anything about the trip home after a day's flying. Nevertheless it seems necessary to me, as I have repeatedly observed a modeller spend a whole Sunday afternoon getting his model correctly set up, finally succeed in making it fly properly, and then suddenly forget all his care when it comes to travelling home, throwing the model into the car boot without thinking that he is destroying his day's work of adjustment.

You really ought to make a conscious effort to hang on to the adjustments and trim positions you have established, so that you have a good chance of starting where you left off when next you go flying. So take care when it comes to packing the rotor away, and note the position of any pushrods which you may have to disconnect for transport. Carefully pack away your accessories.

If any defects have shown up, or you need to replace any item, then make a note of the parts required—using the catalogue or parts list, if possible—and order them right at the start of the week, not when you first have a free moment. The next weekend will come and go, and neither your dealer nor any express transit service can work miracles in getting replacement parts to you.

VII. Flight training

1. General

This chapter is addressed to the complete beginner, i.e. to the fellow who has had no experience of controlling a radio-controlled model helicopter of any type. It is also aimed at anyone who has had experience with a fixed wing aircraft, as these modellers sometimes find it particularly difficult to make the transition to the model helicopter, as they assume that they will gain from their experience with fixed wing aircraft. This assumption is entirely wrong, as the control of a helicopter is quite different from that of a fixed wing aircraft. Of course, certain movements are analogous, e.g. aileron control/lateral cyclic. However, a helicopter's reactions are entirely different, and experience of flying fixed wing is of very little use in this new field. The flyer making the transition from fixed wing to helicopter must be clear about the similarities and differences, and be prepared to begin from the beginning.

When starting initial training, always remember that even the great 'experts' had to make a start at some time or other. They only reached their present level of skill by dint of their determination, and by investing a lot of time, and sometimes an enormous amount of money. With a few exceptions, it usually takes 2 to 3 years for a pilot to really master the model helicopter. So do not expect a miracle; you should not be discouraged if everything does not fall into place at the first attempt. You must be determined and patient if you are to succeed, and if you are, you have already made the important step towards success; you will have a good chance of learning to fly your helicopter in a reasonable length of time.

Just a few more words on the arrangement of the controls:

If you have learned to fly fixed wing models, do not expect your experience to be of much use in learning to fly helicopters, as already mentioned above. However, it is a good idea to keep to the arrangement of controls that you have got accustomed to.

The function you have learned as 'rudder' should be replaced by 'tail rotor' if possible, as both controls have the same effect, viz. course correction around the vertical axis.

The same applies to aileron control. This function is analogous to lateral cyclic control, as both have a similar effect on the respective machines.

At this point we ought to recall briefly the individual control functions:

a) Ascent and descent of the helicopter by operation of the throttle, and thereby altering the main rotor's rotational speed, or by simultaneous operation of the collective pitch control of the main rotor blades.

Fig. 114: The beginner should avoid starting with narrow-based skids on a grass field, if possible. There is a high risk of a skid catching in the grass when the model comes down at an angle, and this will turn the model over (Kavan Alouette).

b) Rotation around the vertical axis, i.e. altering the fuselage heading by altering the tail rotor setting.

c) Lateral tilting of the main rotor around the longitudinal axis, by inclining the swashplate.

d) Inclination of the model forward and backward around the lateral axis, producing forward acceleration and forward flight, or rearward acceleration and rearward flight, by tilting the swashplate forward and back.

The layout of these functions on the transmitter sticks has already been covered in detail in 'Installation of the R/C system'.

155

2. Training stand or free flight?

There are basically two alternative methods of learning to fly a helicopter. The first method is to attach the model to a special training stand, and the second is to proceed immediately to free flight, i.e. with no mechanical restraints.

Fig. 115: A training stand is a very great help for initial training, as all the controls can be practised in absolute safety. It is not quite as easy as this picture shows, admittedly, as it is usually impossible to trim out a helicopter exactly. The model always tends to wander off in one direction or another.

The main advantage of the training stand is that it permits you to practise all the controls without any danger of mishap. You can get used to the helicopter and its handling, as well as learning the correct use of the controls, the right amount of stick movement to apply, and the model's reactions to them. The operation of the tail rotor, and learning how gradually to lift the model off and set it down again, can be learned very well in a training stand, of whatever make. The stand also lets you adjust the motor and run it in without any fears. While you are running in the motor, you have the chance to play with the controls and generally get used to this new kind of flying machine. It is also easy to adjust blade tracking, and find the optimum trim for the tail rotor, and you will find it possible to come to a very good balance between motor throttle, rotor speed, and collective pitch settings. The whole mechanical system can also be checked for smoothness of operation, and any other mechanical checks carried out in complete safety, with the machine still in the training stand. I would always recommend a training stand for the beginner, and it even gives the advanced pilot the opportunity to check the effect of adjustments and repairs without risking the model. Such tests can be carried out without going to the flying field, as long as there are no problems with regard to noise etc. The disadvantage of the training stand is that lateral and pitch control are not easily learned, and these controls can prove deceptive. This applies especially to stands whose pitch and roll pivot is below the model. It is possible to learn the general direction of the control reactions, but not the right amount of control to give. Training stands with a universal joint allow the model to tilt around its centre of gravity. Here the pitch and roll movements (swashplate) can be accurately trimmed out, and the correct amount of control can also be learned. The pilot has to realize that the model would immediately move away from its previous position if it were controlled in the same way in free flight, and would accelerate in the direction of the tilt. This does not happen on the training stand, of course, and to that extent the movements of the model in the stand are deceptive.

It is true to say that the pilot can progress quite a long way with the model in a training stand, provided that he is prepared to analyze his actions. In fact, anyone who is really self-critical and works hard at a training stand until he never makes a mistake with the model, will be able to make the transition to free flight and be successful immediately.

Remember, however, that a training stand has limits on its stability and is not intended for use at full throttle. A helicopter on full power can produce enormous forces and the stand can become unsafe. Quite a lot of people have flown off complete with their stands! Be careful, please.

Learning to fly unrestrained has the undoubted advantage that the pilot can study the model's reactions in actual flight right from the beginning, and he immediately begins to get the feeling of how it reacts to certain pitch and roll commands. It is this characteristic which is the really different aspect of helicopter flying.

Free flight involves a considerable risk of damaging your machine, as the most difficult movements have to be learned with the machine very close to the ground. This leaves extremely little time to correct mistakes before a crash happens. Another factor is that the beginner has relatively little chance of trimming his model out, as there are often just fractions of a second to get it right. A fairly large area will be needed for initial free flight training, as the beginner will find it impossible to control his first test 'hops' to the extent that the machine stays in a confined area.

On the other hand, there are some excellent beginners' aids for learning to fly untethered in the form of special wide-based landing gear or floats. These wide fittings usually look rather inelegant, but they are exceptionally useful, as they allow the beginner to set down his model even when it is banked over, without it tipping right over. For the larger helicopters in particular, floats fixed to an appropriately wide-based landing gear have proved excellent for training, as the floats not only absorb much of the shock of striking the ground, but their rounded contours enable them to slide through grass and over bumpy ground, where skids would tend to get caught up, and turn the model over.

For the smaller makes of helicopter the normal wide-based landing skids have proved better in my experience, as they do not raise the model's centre of gravity unnecessarily high: it is also possible to keep the skids relatively widely spaced. This is not always

Fig. 115a: The Schlüter 'Heli-Trainer' in use. The model is able to rise and sink about 20 cm, turn on its vertical axis and tilt in all directions, using a spring on the undercarriage.

advisable with floats, as they would obtrude into the rotor's downwash and cause a large reduction in rotor thrust.

Also very helpful are two light cross-bars under the skids, length about equal to rotor diameter. On flat ground plain cross-bars are adequate, but on uneven ground, longish grass and so on, tennis balls or similar placed on the ends of the bars will stop them from digging or catching in anything.

3. Learning to fly using a training stand

I am assuming that the pilot has no experience, and is effectively starting from scratch. If you already have some experience of flying a model helicopter, feel free to miss out some of the stages in training that are suggested.

For this first phase only train on the tail rotor and vertical up and down movement, which will give you the feel of things for starting a hover. It doesn't matter if the model has collective or non-collective pitch control. Block the model to prevent forward, backward or sideways tilt—it should only be able to move straight up and down and rotate about its axis.

Start up the motor, as described in the previous chapter, and take all the starting accessories and cleaning rags etc. out of the way of the rotor.

Check that nothing and nobody can get in your way or get into the path of the spinning rotor blades (onlookers, children, animals, other models' wings blown into the air, sheets of balsa leaning against the garage wall etc. . . !).

Now advance the throttle *slowly, and with feeling,* to increase the rotor's speed. You will notice immediately that the machine starts to rotate, and the skids will slide to and fro on the platform. Try to stop this rotation with the tail rotor, and hold the helicopter straight. Always fly with the model heading directly away from you.

You must stop yourself watching the tail rotor—it is of no interest to you! Watch the centre of the model, and impress on your mind the movements 'left means *nose* to the left, right means *nose* to the right'. This is vital!

Now play with the throttle/rotor speed control (or collective pitch), and try to acquire a feeling for the changes in torque. Always correct the model's heading. With the throttle advanced so that the skids are sliding about, attempt intentional turns to left and right

159

Fig. 116:
If you use a training stand which incorporates a universal joint mounting for the helicopter at the centre of gravity, the control reactions will correspond very closely to free flight. You should bear in mind that the model would fly off at high speed to the left in free flight if inclined as shown here.

using tail rotor. You can also try 'flying' to left, to right, towards you etc.

Now advance the throttle/pitch progressively until the model starts to lift off. Don't forget to check and correct the model's heading! Fly up until the top stop is reached, and check out the throttle setting and adjustment of the motor.

Now back down again; reduce throttle/pitch very gradually — not too much — hold heading, set it down gently. Throttle back to idle, do not let the machine turn away from you. Have a breather. Once again from the beginning, but slowly. Throttle forward, hold the heading etc. etc. You know the sequence now.

Continue practising constantly, until the functions of 'up/down' and 'tail rotor' are second nature to you. Even in blustery weather and in a strong wind. Turn to the left, towards yourself etc. From time to time ask yourself what you would do if a sudden gust of wind arrived. Always keep a check on altitude and heading. Try flying at half height too!

At this stage you can also let your wife/girl friend, daughter, son, flying colleague or spectator take control. There is no danger, and everyone will enjoy it. You will also quickly notice anyone who has developed a special feeling for controlling models. Many an absolute beginner masters this stage of helicopter flying in just a few minutes.

Now it gets more difficult. In our attempts so far, the model has only been allowed to rise and fall vertically, and rotate around its vertical axis. Now the lateral movement facility of the training stand is released. The model can now tilt to left and right, and you should repeat all the previous practice sessions, while trying to hold the model level laterally. This is by no means so easy, as you now have to control three functions at once.

You will notice that you can easily 'forget' one control in this situation, because you have been concentrating too hard on one movement in particular. This is quite natural, and is a part of the learning process. Tilt the helicopter to one side deliberately, and correct again with short powerful commands in the opposite direction. When hovering, try to correct every small lateral movement immediately. If you cannot recognize the horizontal position easily, attach a strip of balsa across the skids; this will show up the smallest rolling movement. Always try and counteract these movements immediately and precisely, and maintain the correct height and heading.

Fig. 117: An extreme rearward inclination like this would result in an immediate reversal of direction.

RCHM-F

Practise this again and again, but please not with full power or the rotor at maximum pitch.

Now you are ready to release the pitch facility, enabling the model to tilt forward and backward. Carry on practising, as described before, using all four functions. You are now flying 'on all axes', and you will have both hands full. You have to carry out four things all at the same time: maintain your height, maintain heading, control lateral attitude, and keep a check on pitch attitude.

Unfortunately a model helicopter does not do the pilot the favour of moving exactly to one side, or exactly forward. It will tilt forward and to one side, forward and left, rearward and left etc. You have to counteract these movements by combined control in roll and pitch. This is by no means easy initially, and here it helps if you can get away from the idea that the swashplate is operated by two functions. Consider the main rotor's movement (and hence the model's) as a single movement, and give corresponding control commands. Try deliberately to learn how the helicopter tilts relative to its forward heading, and try to forget that the movement is made up of so much roll and so much pitch.

The learning of pitch and roll control can be made much easier by locking the stand a few centimetres high, thereby keeping the skids in the air. The helicopter is now freely suspended, without the skids touching the platform, and you can practise pitch and roll control at a low throttle setting. If you have trouble with the helicopter rotating on its vertical axis during this stage, and this confuses you, you can block this movement in any convenient way. Now you can really concentrate on pitch and roll control.

You must not allow yourself to become complacent when practising in the training stand. To date no experts have leapt down from heaven ready made, and helicopter flying, although quite fascinating, is by no means easy. Take regular breaks from practising, switch off for a while, and do not try to force the pace. Nobody masters the art in one weekend. Above all, learn to be critical of yourself. If your machine still gets out of control occasionally, it is best to carry on practising on the training stand. Let somebody else take control, and watch what mistakes he makes. That helps too. Try walking 10 metres from the training stand, and control from a distance. This will give you a certain amount of confidence for subsequent free flying, when you will not always be close by the model. At this stage you can find out what it looks like when the model is heading towards you at a distance of 10 m, or is travelling away from you, or if it flies off to right or left. Always bear in mind that you have to keep the model absolutely horizontal, and the slightest tilt in any direction must be deliberately corrected.

When you can manage all this without difficulty, and without making obvious errors, then you have learned practically everything needed for free flying. The only thing which you do not know now is the speed with which the helicopter will move off when the rotor is tilted, and in which direction the model will move. What you should have mastered by now is the control inputs necessary to counter any tilt or rotation, without getting into difficulties with the other functions, or even losing your nerve and giving the wrong commands. This initial mastery of the basic principles is the vital prerequisite if you are to be successful in free flying from the start. You can now go on confidently to your first untethered take-off. This does not mean that you will be able to fly circuits straight off; you are not an expert helicopter flyer yet.

Bear a few points in mind before you start:

You will have been practising on the training stand with narrow-based skids. If you have a large, smooth strip, you can safely carry on using the narrow undercarriage. If you only have a grass field available, wider-based skids or even floats are better.

Before you take off for the first time, check again that all functions are working correctly. Check blade tracking, smooth running, radio functions and motor settings. Check that there is enough

Fig. 118:
For your first 'hops' in free flight, especially over rough ground, floats have proved to be ideal. They not only provide a shock-absorbing effect on hard landings, but they are able to slide over clumps of grass and uneven ground when the model is moving sideways.

fuel in the tank (!), that the aerial has not been ripped out during practice (!) and that you are also fit and ready to go . . . . .

Is anybody dangerously close?

Now you should be ready for your first free hovering flight. Imagine you are still on the training stand. Advance the throttle/pitch slowly, maintain heading, do not let the tail rotate. Stand behind the model, take it up to at least 30 cm., and 50 cm. or 1 m. for preference. Don't forget all you have learned in the excitement! If the model tilts over and is about to fly off in that direction, counter the movement with an adequately powerful, but properly regulated, amount of opposite control, just as when practising. These correcting commands should be brief, but powerful, so that you can see your model's reaction as quickly as possible, now that it is not tethered. Try to keep the model stationary. Whether this occurs right in front of you, or maybe 10 or 20 m away, is not important at first. *Whatever happens, follow the model,* so that you do not have to correct unwanted flight movements from a distance of 20 or 30 m. You will not be used to this, and it involves an unnecessary risk.

If you are not sure of yourself, set the model down, just as on the training stand. Try to maintain the model's heading by giving short but powerful commands, as the model descends (you should know

Fig. 119: The landing gear can also be effectively widened by attaching strips of wood, for flying over rough ground.

164

immediately which way to turn the model by now), and land the model more or less gently. Of course, you should try to carry out the landing by pulling back the throttle relatively slowly (or reducing collective pitch equally slowly), even in an emergency. Sudden throttle changes nearly always result in the model rotating rapidly, and suddenly the model is pointing in the opposite direction, and the controls are reversed.

At this point I have a few more words for the advanced pilot: a training stand can be a great help to the advanced flyer. Before flying a new model, for example, you can attach the helicopter to the training stand, check the trim settings, adjust or correct the full throttle setting, and you can be more confident at the first proper take-off. Perhaps the biggest advantage is that you can usually carry out a brief test flight in this way close to your home, avoiding a long drive to the actual flying field. The experienced flyer can also practise the more difficult hovering manoeuvres. For instance, it is not at all easy to fly a helicopter directly towards yourself, even for experienced flyers. Virtually all the controls are reversed, and the model when seen from the front often looks completely different. However, this manoeuvre can be learned perfectly using a training stand, and the model's reactions will be practically identical to free flight. This works better if the model's support system is a good one; a fully articulated suspension is a great help here, as the helicopter can move around its own centre of gravity, and its movements therefore correspond very closely to free flight.

Another possible use for a training stand is at modelling displays. The platform can serve as an exhibition stand and the helicopter can be rotated and viewed from all sides. If you wish to explain the flying controls to an interested public, the model can easily be suspended in the stand, allowing all the flight and control movements to be explained and demonstrated.

If the situation allows, a very good flying demonstration can be carried out in the stand; the public can even be allowed to have a 'fly'. It is best to lock the pitch and roll facilities of the stand, so that the helicopter can only rise and descend, and rotate on its vertical axis. These two functions can be learned relatively quickly by a newcomer, and he will get quite a feeling of accomplishment. You will not need full power in the training stand, so you can add extra silencing. For example, a length of exhaust tubing, or a large auxiliary silencer, have a marked effect on the noise level, making it possible to operate the machine in quite an enclosed space.

You could, of course, take the matter further, and hold a real 'competition' for the public. There are numerous possibilities here, and it is very interesting to see how many people are attracted by this fascinating 'toy', and who may then be 'hooked' by model flying.

It is *absolutely vital* that you insist on *absolute safety* for all practice flights and experiments involving a training stand. A helicopter attached to a training stand looks quite harmless, and the spinning rotor blades are often not noticed. This even applies to other model flyers at the flying site, but is especially so amongst laymen at a display. Keep the public at a safe distance by barriers, if possible down to the ground, for it is more than annoying when suddenly your neighbour's dog appears and starts a fight with the rotor blades. And then when the dog's young master comes running after him, matters start to get out of hand.

4. Free flight practice

All the advice on starting the motor, checking blade tracking, checking all the other functions etc., given in the previous chapters, applies equally to untethered practice. The following important points should also be borne in mind.

Always fly with extra wide and long skids, so that the model's ground contact area is as great as possible. In the initial training period this area cannot be too large, and you should not let yourself be limited by the look of the thing.

These notes apply equally to collective or non-collective pitch control models. Reference to 'throttle' means 'pitch' for this purpose, i.e. increasing throttle can be taken as increasing pitch, depending on the model.

For initial free flight practice, it is very important that the motor is correctly adjusted, and that the rest of the rotor system functions perfectly. Obviously, it is absolutely essential that the motor is adjusted correctly at its full throttle setting, and to do this you will either need an assistant to hold the model above his head, or you will need to fix the model to a trestle or table or something similar. Obviously, great care needs to be taken with regard to the spinning rotor blades (and the tail rotor), and you should make sure that no flying colleagues or curious onlookers come too close.

When you have adjusted the full throttle, idle and intermediate settings as described above, and have checked blade tracking, you can take the model down from the table or trestle. Do be sure not to get up, or lift the model from the table, until the rotor blades have actually stopped! Apart from the fact that there is a lot of energy in the spinning rotor system, you risk altering the blade settings.

Your next task is to find a piece of ground for your first 'hops' which is as open as possible, and you will need space in all directions. Consider that a helicopter can fly not only forwards and backwards, but can also fly straight towards you; you will need space behind you if that happens. So under no circumstances take off close by the take-off strip or your colleagues' models, and, obviously, not immediately in front of spectators.

Carry out the final checks, as described earlier, concerning adequate fuel, extended aerial, proper operation of all four functions, and whether the air and the take-off strip are free for you to make your first attempts. Is your frequency free?

Now comes the first stage, in which the tail rotor has to be trimmed out. It is best if the model is on as smooth a surface as possible, so that it will start skidding about at a low throttle setting, i.e. when the throttle is advanced gently, the model will rotate without coming clear of the ground. This gives you the chance to control the tail rotor. Slowly advance the throttle until the machine gets light on its skids, and appears to 'swim' about on the ground. Now you can tell if the model is trying to rotate around its vertical axis. If the tail rotor is set up exactly according to the manufacturer's instructions, you are sure to be able to trim out any rotation on the transmitter trim lever. Continue trying to trim out the tail rotor

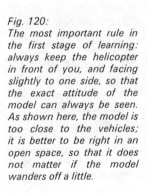

Fig. 120:
The most important rule in the first stage of learning: always keep the helicopter in front of you, and facing slightly to one side, so that the exact attitude of the model can always be seen. As shown here, the model is too close to the vehicles; it is better to be right in an open space, so that it does not matter if the model wanders off a little.

Fig. 121:
That's better: completely unobstructed land all around,
and a hard surface (asphalt
or concrete). In this case you
can afford to use a narrower-
based set of skids, as there is
virtually no danger of the
skids 'catching' on landing.

Fig. 122: You can, of course, fly over rough ground with relatively narrow-based skids,
but you should be sufficiently skilled to land the model squarely. This is quite feasible
if you can keep the model precisely in front of you and set it down from there.

until the model no longer shows a definite tendency to turn in a particular direction when you keep the model very close to the ground. However, do note the wind direction, and keep the model's nose into the wind. Watch out for any changes in wind direction during your flight tests. If the transmitter trim lever does not have enough movement to trim out the tail rotor, you will have to alter the tail rotor linkage or the servo throw to correct the situation.

These first attempts at hovering are solely for the purpose of setting the tail rotor trim, and for getting the first 'feel' of how the helicopter behaves. Before starting actual flight tests, you should read through the basic flying rules, described in some detail in the next section.

5. The basic flying rules

Basic rule No. 1: Never fix the model to the ground.

The model should never simply be tied to the ground by string or something similar. The model must be free to move in all directions, otherwise the main rotor stabilisation system cannot work properly. Restraining the model in this way frustrates all its natural movements, as the helicopter loses its balance at the moment when its movement is blocked by the string. What is more, the pilot would immediately be called upon to carry out the most difficult manoeuvre of all, that is flying precisely over one spot. That is too much to ask at the first attempt. If you consider restraint is needed, then you should practise using a training stand, as described earlier.

Basic rule No. 2: Keep the model's nose pointing into wind.

Make sure that the model's nose always points directly into wind, especially when you are first learning. You should never attempt to take off with a crosswind, even if it looks very easy, or if the wind is very light. If the tail rotor is trimmed correctly, the model will turn to face the wind immediately after take-off, and the beginner will then find it difficult to keep track of this rotation, and react correctly to it. Taking off downwind is downright disastrous, as the model nearly always turns through 180 degrees, totally confusing the pilot.

Basic rule No. 3: Walk along with the model

Always walk along following the model, especially right at the start.

RCHM–F*

Fig. 123: One bad example presented here as a warning: checking motor settings while holding onto the tail of the model. The pilot's fingers are very likely to be injured by the tail rotor, and if the main rotor is over-controlled by mistake, the tail could come out of his grasp.

Ideally you should keep the helicopter about 5 m away from you—the nose pointing into wind, of course. Take off slowly, and let the model fly smoothly in any direction. Don't stay glued to the spot; walk along with the model, always aiming to keep the same distance away from it. The model can be observed much more easily if it is not too far away. You will also have the advantage that you are looking in the same direction as the model is pointing.

Basic rule No. 4: Forget the tail rotor

Very important. The tail rotor and the fin should be completely ignored in normal flight. The centre of the fuselage and the nose are the parts to watch. As with a normal fixed wing aircraft, a left turn around the vertical axis is produced by moving the stick left, without considering that the model's tail moves to the right. A surprising number of model flyers make the mistake of not watching the model's direction of flight, that is, controlling the nose's heading, but just watch the tail rotor. The result is that the tail rotor turns to the left, and a command of 'right' is given to compensate, which is, of course, incorrect. This reversed method of control can be learned almost to perfection, which inevitably leads to a complete fiasco, probably during your first circuit. At that time, with the model a good few metres away, you will give a reversed command, and a crash is just about inevitable. Always remember that the tail rotor works just like a fixed wing model's rudder.

Basic rule No. 5: Operate the motor throttle or collective pitch control slowly and gently

Whenever you open or close the throttle, or alter the collective pitch setting, there is a corresponding change in torque. Provided that you operate these controls slowly and gently, these torque variations stay within limits, and can be recognized early enough to be compensated for.

Basic rule No. 6: Don't be afraid of a banked attitude

A certain degree of bank or tilt is absolutely harmless, as long as the model is free to fly off in that direction without striking the ground. It is a common mistake to assume that a model will always tend to tip over in this situation. This is not true, as long as the model can be kept a reasonable height above ground, and is not suddenly braked by one skid touching the ground; this would forcibly tip the model over. If the model is hovering, it will accelerate off in the direction of the inclination of the rotor head, and the situation then calls for you carefully to apply opposite control to stop this movement. Timid flyers frequently lose their nerve at this point and close the throttle; the model lands banked over, resulting in a crash. It is much easier to open the throttle slightly, so that at least the model stays airborne, and gives you time to apply the appropriate control to correct the tilt.

Basic rule No. 7: Learn to hover first

This rule is important, because it will save you from unnecessary disappointments. You must practise hovering until you can do it confidently, as it is the start and finish of all other manoeuvres. Also, the relatively low altitude maintained in hovering practice means that you can set the model down at any time, if you give a wrong command, or get into difficulties. This at least avoids the danger of serious damage.

Basic rule No. 8: If you land banked over, immediately close the throttle

During initial training in hovering flight, you are bound to make mistakes, and it will seem the best idea to land the model from the low height of hovering practice. In this case, you must reduce the throttle as slowly as possible, and also try to keep the model straight, i.e. horizontal, without a skidding motion, for the touch-down. This will not always work out, however, and occasionally the helicopter will land while skidding sideways. In this situation, as soon as the model touches the ground, you must chop the throttle straight down to idle (or reduce collective pitch to minimum), contrary to all I have said so far, so that no lift is being produced. Otherwise the machine will be balanced on one skid, and its own excess rotor thrust may turn it over. Ground effect also provides a marked increase in thrust as you get close to the ground, which also increases the danger of turning over.

Basic rule No. 9: Observe the difference between fuselage and rotor

The main rotor of a helicopter is controlled by the swashplate. This means that the main rotor always follows the movement of the swashplate, and it makes no difference whether the swashplate is tilted by a deliberate control input, or it is following an inclination of the fuselage without any command being applied. The main rotor does not differentiate between a movement of the swashplate caused by a control signal and one caused by the fuselage banking.

This is how it works: If the fuselage is exactly horizontal, and you tilt the swashplate forward by 3 degrees, the main rotor disc will also tilt forward by 3 degrees. The result is that the fuselage accelerates forward strongly. This acceleration causes the fuselage to assume an angle of inclination of perhaps 2 degrees. If you maintain the 3 degree swashplate tilt, this setting will now be added to the fuselage inclination of 2 degrees, so that the swashplate now assumes a forward tilt of 5 degrees compared with its original position. The rotor now follows the swashplate, and goes from 3 degrees forward tilt to 5 degrees forward. Acceleration increases, generally to an undesirable extent. To brake the forward flight it will not be enough to neutralise the swashplate (i.e. return the cyclic pitch control stick on the transmitter to neutral). If the fuselage is tilted forward by 2 degrees, the swashplate is also tilted forward by that amount. The main rotor will stay at 2 degrees forward, and the model will continue accelerating forwards, although at a reduced rate. To bring the model to a halt, you will need to incline the swashplate backward by 2 degrees, to override the fuselage tilt. Now the swashplate will be back in its earlier horizontal position, and the main rotor will also be horizontal, and thus produce no more horizontal acceleration. To stop forward flight, the main rotor must be inclined rearward. Returning to our situation where the total forward inclination was 3 degrees (swashplate) plus 2 degrees (fuselage), the actual swashplate movement required is 5 degrees rearward, applied from the transmitter stick.

Basic rule No. 10: Don't be put off

Don't be put off by the above explanation. Controlling a model helicopter is not exactly straightforward, but it generally sounds much worse than it is in practice. Of course, all this is entirely new territory for the beginner, and sometimes he will not find it easy to keep all the balls in the air at once and always give the right control input. I would strongly recommend you to read and re-read these basic rules, and try to think through what you have to do in this or that situation before you actually make your first flight. It can be a great help at this stage to watch other helicopter pilots, though when watching an expert it is difficult to imagine just how much intensive practice lies behind his skill. Hard practice is essential to mastery of any skill, be it helicopter flying, fixed wing flying, or any other technical skill. Do remember that everyone has to start right from the beginning, and that you will not look a fool if you have to start with rather pathetic and primitive little hops.

Basic rule No. 11: Don't be talked into anything

This last rule is of special importance. It happens again and again

Fig. 124: Initial training.
A. A good starting position. An adequate distance from the model, a light headwind, nose of the model into wind, slow advance of throttle, maintain heading with tail rotor, and allow the model to lift off. Now wait and see what happens.

that other model flyers get fed up with seeing you head off for a corner of the field with your helicopter, to practise the same old test hops again and again. These people are not directly involved, and they will not be able to share the feelings of personal achievement or satisfaction felt by the pilot when he feels that he is beginning to master his model after a few practice sessions. Usually it is not long before you get a friendly suggestion, or even a more or less direct challenge, to show what this helicopter business is all about, and fly a proper circuit for once. This is likely to end in great disappointment, and the wreckage is usually left for *you* to repair, not for your friends. The moral is: Do not let anyone talk you into any manoeuvre which you have not mastered yet. Just keep on practising, and keep telling yourself that there is nothing to stop your colleagues buying a helicopter, and showing you how it is done.

6. Initial training

As already stated, it is advisable to make your first attempts on a wide open, unobstructed space, and a smooth surface is a great help. The weather should not be too blustery, but a light, smooth breeze is a definite advantage, preferably from a steady direction. Place the model down with its nose pointing into wind, and stand about 5 m behind the machine. Now advance the throttle, very

B. The model is beginning to incline backwards very slowly. Can you see that? If you can, you are already an advanced pilot, and need only push the stick forward briefly (forward cyclic), and the model will continue hovering in the same position.

slowly, and in small increments. Let the clutch engage smoothly, and slowly raise the rotor speed. Keep advancing the throttle until the machine gets light on its skids and begins to 'swim' about. If your model has collective pitch control, raise motor speed to maximum, and wait for the first reaction while slowly and smoothly pulling 'up'. When the model starts to skid about, concentrate on holding the model into wind by trimming out the tail rotor. When this is under control, advance the throttle a little further until the model begins to lift off. Only one notch at a time! When rotor speed has risen and reached a constant speed, ground effect will very rapidly build up. Keep a very close watch on the model during these initial hops, to find out whether it has a tendency to tilt to one side or another. If so, alter the cyclic control trims. Initially you can use the transmitter trims to cancel out these tendencies, but if the trims are not sufficient to compensate, you will have to adjust the appropriate pushrod in the helicopter.

When you think that the model is no longer trying to fly off in a particular direction (observe the angle of the fuselage carefully here), then advance the throttle slightly again, until the model is hovering about 20–50 cm up. At this height the model will usually settle on a cushion of air, although it is likely to try to move off in one direction or another. You must recognize this tendency at once, and try to apply the appropriate counter-control to the main rotor to neutralize the tilt of the machine. Don't stay rooted to the spot, but walk along with the model, always trying to

C. If you are not that experienced, you will reach this position. You notice the rearward inclination a little later, and the model is now beginning to fly backwards and lose height. Now you have no choice: stick forward sharply (strong forward cyclic). If you do not do this, in the next moment the model will turn through 180° and head straight for you with its nose down.

keep the model's nose into the wind. There is absolutely no need to fly the model back to the take-off point; the only important thing is to keep the movement in any direction slow, and keep the machine in hovering flight. Whether you manage to stop its movement in 3 m, 5 m, 10 m, or even 20 m is neither here nor there. Now you will see why it is important to have enough space around your take-off point in all directions, as the model can fly not only forwards, but just as easily backwards towards you. During these first attempts to stop the model wandering off, you must realize that a certain amount of time is needed to slow down and stop this movement. Generally speaking, it is best to give brief, but relatively powerful and definite stick movements, so that you can see the model's reaction, and therefore get a better idea of how to stop unwanted movement.

These first attempts at lifting off, hovering and correcting movement should be repeated over and over. Try to prevent the model skidding round sideways, by holding the nose into the wind, and you will see what a help a constant wind can be. The model will have a quite pronounced weather-cocking effect, and will relieve you of at least part of the worry of controlling the tail rotor.

When you have successfully completed these test flights many times, you will have developed a feeling for arresting and correcting the model. You will then be in a position to let the model climb to 1 m, or even 1.5 or 2.0 m and try again. At this stage—provided that you are not still making basic control errors—you should remember not to close the throttle (or reduce collective pitch) in flight when you make a slight mistake, which would cause the model to crash

D. The 'forward' command has worked. Although the model has lost some height and has moved downwind, it is back in the correct attitude.

to the ground. You will never learn to fly a helicopter like that. It is much better to try and maintain altitude and coolly apply the appropriate corrections, even if the result is a zig-zagging flight over the entire flying field. But do remember not to stay fixed to the spot; *always* walk along with your model. Get that idea firmly fixed in your mind. If you find that you forget to do this out of sheer excitement and concentration on the model, then tell one of your flying colleagues to remind you every time you appear to be nailed down to one spot, while your helicopter gets further and further away.

During these attempts you will notice one thing, and that is that the model flies much more smoothly as soon as it leaves the area of ground effect, i.e. when it climbs from about 50 cm−1 m up to about 2 m. Ground effect has less influence at that height, and the model will usually no longer have that pronounced tendency to fly off to one side.

Do not be tempted to fly circuits when you are at this first stage, even if it looks likely to happen whether you want it or not. It will be completely unnerving for you suddenly to see the model sideways on, as all the flight movements are quite different from the new viewpoint; this will thoroughly confuse you at first. As soon as you have the model under reasonable control, it is much better to keep the model's nose into the wind and steer it deliberately to left

E. *But now the machine is heading off to the right. Don't panic and close the throttle; apply a brief, powerful command of 'left cyclic' and open the throttle slightly. The model will continue to the right for a little way, but will eventually stop, gaining a little height.*

and right and back again. You can allow these excursions to either side to go further each time, and without climbing to more than 5 m, move to right and left, hover in various places etc. You can also try pushing on forward into the wind by pushing the stick forward a little, and fly forward for 10, 15 or 20 m. But always keep the model heading into wind, and alternately move to left and right and back again. If the wind is strong, you will be able to let the wind carry the model back towards you in this way, with the heading always the same, until it is close to you again. Then reduce the throttle very slowly (or reduce collective pitch slowly), until you can land the model back close to you.

These hovering flights should be repeated over and over again, and you should avoid being persuaded into trying a circuit even yet. At this stage a circuit would probably start well, and you might even feel that you are over the hardest part. You would be right too, as you should really have mastered hovering by the end of this stage.

If you are quite sure of everything so far, there is no reason why you should not advance the throttle further (or increase collective pitch) until you are up to a height of 8 to 10 m. Still keep the nose heading into wind, and the model in front of you. Climbing like this should be carried out in very gentle stages, to prevent the

F. That's it! Lateral movement is arrested. Now the nose is slightly down and the model wants to pick up speed forward. Don't let it happen. Back cyclic, but neutralize again as soon as the nose rises.

helicopter getting too high too soon, which might make you panic. It will feel very strange to be looking up and across at the model, and if the model arrives directly overhead, you will find it very difficult to judge vertical movement. So it is better to keep the model about 10 or 15m in front of you at this stage, so that you are always looking at the rear three-quarter view of your machine. This will enable you to judge height much better. Now try and bring the model down again by reducing the throttle/collective pitch setting. It is vital here to reduce the setting very slowly and smoothly, to avoid the machine picking up vertical speed in its descent. Then you would need to open the throttle quickly (or increase collective pitch), which would result in a rapid increase in torque with resultant loss of control as the tail swings round. Bear in mind also that the model can drop into its own rotor downwash, which spells disaster. So—when hovering at a fair height, allow the model to descend very deliberately, using extremely delicate control movements, and keep a constant check on wind direction. Don't let the excitement of the situation make you forget your lateral movements; try to keep the model diagonally in front of you.

The same rules apply to these flights: definite, but relatively brief control inputs, watch for the model's attitude changing, and then

G. *Everything in order again. Any moment now the model will tilt over in one direction or another. Will you pick it up in time? If not, then land the model at this stage by slowly closing the throttle. Time for a break. Now do it all over again!*

wait for the reaction in flight direction. You must always realize that it takes a certain amount of time for any particular movement to be arrested.

Here is an example: your model is hovering at a height of 2–3 m. The fuselage begins to tilt backwards, barely noticeably; later on, you will know that backwards flight will result from this, and you will apply opposite control to prevent it happening. However, at first your reaction will come too late, and the model will begin flying backwards. Now you tilt the main rotor forward by pushing the swashplate stick forward strongly and definitely. Hold this command on until the fuselage is once more horizontal, or tilted very slightly forward. Now you must take off the control immediately, or the model will instantly start moving in exactly the opposite direction, i.e. forwards, and will accelerate in this direction. When the model has stopped and is again stationary, lift the model's nose slightly until the fuselage is absolutely horizontal. Perhaps the model is now a few metres downwind of its original position—you did walk back with it, didn't you?—but at least it is stationary again. Now try to compensate for this unwanted movement by deliberately pushing forward again to the original spot. Give a short forward cyclic input to push the nose down, and the model will slowly incline forwards and begin to fly in that direction. Before it reaches too high a speed, neutralise the swashplate and slow the helicopter down. All the movements of the helicopter are controlled in this way, and you should try and fix in your mind this sequence:

a) Stop the movement.

b) Initiate movement in the opposite direction.

c) Stop the movement again.

d) Maintain the new position.

This procedure corresponds exactly to the control of every fullsize helicopter.

7. Advanced training

When you have really mastered hovering flight as described in the preceding sections, and have not completed a circuit already by accident, it is time to start advanced training, i.e. to try an intentional circuit. Is there still some fuel in the tank?

Lift the model off into hover at about 2 m altitude. Trim the model out as precisely as possible, and fly crosswind a few times to get used to hovering again, and to settle your nerves. After doing this for 2 or 3 minutes, with the model completely under control, you will know that your motor is running correctly, and that all the mechanical systems are in order.

Now tilt the nose forward very gently (forward cyclic for just a moment), and head the model forward. You have practised that often enough by now, but have always stopped the movement at that point, to avoid leaving the flying site. Now you leave the throttle/collective pitch where it is (in slow forward flight, extra power is not needed). The model will accelerate forwards, and you will see that the machine tends to fly in a wide curve. The direction will vary according to make, and depends basically on the direction of rotation of the main rotor. Let us assume that it begins flying a right hand turn. At low speed this turn will be very gentle. If you want to be quite sure, allow the model to carry on flying like this, and it will perform a right-hand circuit without much help from you, finishing into wind once again, and fairly close to you. I am assuming, of course, that the wind is very light, and the model is not blown a long way downwind. I am also assuming that the model has not picked up too much speed by being tilted forward too steeply. Should this be the case, raise the nose by pulling up on the main rotor joystick. The machine will react by slowing down, but you should not take this to the extent that the model stops a long distance from you. It is likely to be difficult for you to control the model in hover at such a distance. For this reason you should aim at achieving a steady, but not too fast, forward speed by an appropriate forward inclination of the model.

Basically, you stop the model turning by operating the tail rotor and lateral cyclic simultaneously. At first you will fly a meandering course, but that does not matter, as you have a lot of time in which to correct.

So why does a helicopter fly a turn when it flies forward, instead of flying dead straight?

The main rotor and tail rotor are trimmed for stationary hovering flight. For example, the tail rotor has to compensate for the whole of the main rotor's torque, and it is not assisted by the fin. As forward speed increases, the fin encounters the airstream and provides additional stabilisation. Now the tail rotor is being assisted by the fin, so that its compensating effect is too powerful; the result is that the fuselage will turn to left or right about its vertical axis, depending on the direction of rotation of the main rotor. The tail rotor thrust therefore needs to be reduced by reducing its pitch. Keep a watch on the model's nose and heading. Avoid the common error of trying to correct the tail rotor at this stage. You will apply the wrong control! Do you remember Basic Rule No. 4?

A degree of turn is also produced during forward flight by the asymmetrical airflow over the main rotor. If the main rotor is rotating clockwise, (seen from above) a gentle roll to the right will occur, and vice versa. The reason for this is that the advancing blade (on the left-hand side of a clockwise rotating rotor) is travelling *into* the wind, while the other blade is travelling *downwind*. In other words, the left-hand blade 'sees' a headwind, and the right-hand blade 'sees' a tailwind. Obviously, the right-hand blade will produce less lift than the left-hand blade, with a resulting rolling motion to the right. This rolling tendency increases with increasing forward speed, and has to be countered with an appropriate amount of left cyclic (swashplate tilted left). If the rotor rotates counter-clockwise, the rolling tendency will be to the left, and will have to be compensated for by 'right cyclic' (swashplate tilted to the right). These characteristics are found in full-size helicopters in exactly the same form.

Fig. 125: Circuit practice.
A. Correct: take-off away from the pilot into the wind, climbing steadily. Don't speed up too much.

182

B. *Correct: Obliquely from behind, the model can be observed well. Any inclination laterally or fore and aft can be seen, as also any climb.*

C. *Correct: Flying past you at a good height and a fair distance from the pilot, so that the flight attitude can be watched. The large floats are a great help here.*

183

D. *Wrong: The model is coming straight at the pilot. At this stage he cannot see the fuselage's attitude, and it is possible that the model will lose speed without him knowing, suddenly turn through 180° and fly off in the opposite direction with the nose well down.*

E. *Correct: Landing approach into the wind, coming obliquely from behind. Fore/aft and lateral inclination can be picked up easily, flying speed and sinking speed can be judged well.*

184

F. Correct: Landing approach continues with gradual reduction in sinking speed clearly observed. The shadow is a help here, as it gives a good idea how high up the model is.

G. Correct: Final stage of the landing approach. You are back in the familiar position obliquely behind the model, and are able to exploit your hovering experience. The model is allowed to glide forward slowly and land neatly on its floats. Here too the shadow gives a good indication of altitude.

185

H. Wrong: Landing approach directly towards the pilot. From this point of view the pilot finds it hard to tell the fuselage attitude, and he has more or less no idea of sinking speed and forward speed. This is also the most likely situation for the pilot to confuse 'left' with 'right'. The solution: jump to one side, open the throttle slowly, fly past yourself and try to find the right approach after another large circuit.

Now back to that first circuit:

Your model is now about 20 or 30 m away from you, and you want to initiate a deliberate turn. If it is to be a right-hand turn, and your rotor turns clockwise, you need only neutralise the tail rotor and the lateral tilt of the main rotor. The model will react by flying a turn to the right virtually on its own, as already described. If you want to fly to the left, increase the tail rotor setting and lateral cyclic. Your tail rotor must be capable of a zero degree pitch setting, otherwise the model will not be able to fly a left-hand turn. Usually the tail rotor has to be capable of at least minus 2 or 3 degrees, as otherwise a left turn at high speed will not be possible. (This applies to clockwise rotating systems. For counter-clockwise rotation, the exact opposite is true.)

When flying a turn, the model helicopter tends to lose height exactly as does a fixed wing model. To compensate for this, the nose has to be raised by applying backward cyclic (swashplate back gently), just like applying up elevator. All these controls are

186

fairly straightforward, as the model's response is relatively slow, and you generally have plenty of time to think. A slight amount of under- or over-control is not critical at a reasonable height.

At this point a word of caution: recognizing a helicopter's precise attitude when it is sideways on to you is not all that easy, as it has no fixed wing to act as an aid to orientation when the model is banked over. If the model is not watched very attentively, it can become difficult to tell whether the model is rolling towards you or away from you. If in doubt, give a short, powerful lateral command, and the model's reaction will indicate its actual attitude. The duller the weather, and the smaller the helicopter, the more difficult it is to recognize the model's attitude when it is a fair distance away. For this reason, the radius of operation in which small helicopters can safely be controlled is definitely limited. Many an 'inexplicable' crash at a distance has been caused not by interference or a technical fault, but by an incorrect control input when it was impossible to judge the real flight attitude of the machine.

When you have completed your first turn, the machine will already be fairly high up, if you have not throttled back or reduced collective pitch. Now you have to maintain this altitude by reducing the throttle setting/collective pitch. The model's reaction to throttle control will be a great surprise at first, as hover practice has accustomed you to thinking that a fairly high throttle setting is always

Fig. 126:
Advanced practice: hang a tennis ball underneath the skids on a 1 m long piece of string. Two balsa sticks for the goal. Try to take the ball between the goalposts while hovering.

Fig. 127:
Advanced training: using a large wire sphere (lamp shade frame); attach a 1.5m cord to the model, with a simple wire double hook on the bottom end (the cord must be releasable). In hovering flight, fly up to the sphere, catch it on the hook, lift the sphere into the air, fly a circuit (not too fast, or the sphere will swing from side to side). After the circuit, release the line at the starting position and let the sphere down.

needed, but in forward flight the throttle setting can be reduced quite substantially. Normal circuits are flown virtually at half throttle, or with much reduced collective pitch. This is the result of the extra lift provided by the rotor blades in the airflow caused by forward flight.

If you have a model with speed pre-selection, then trimming is not quite the same as, correctly adjusted, the rotor speed remains constant. If the model flies level it will be very fast and to maintain a steady height at slower speed the pitch will need to be reduced. The rotor will at first speed up due to delay in change of motor r.p.m. but the pitch/throttle will adjust engine speed, down to possibly only half throttle.

It is a good idea now to fly a few triumphal circuits, during which you should try to maintain as even a speed as possible by controlling the fuselage's forward inclination. If you concentrate on this aspect, nothing can really go wrong, as it is quite irrelevant at first whether you end up exactly where you intended, or whether you get blown downwind slightly. Just make sure that the model does not get too far away.

Always approach into wind for the landing. Throttle back further, or reduce collective pitch, towards the end of the circuit, so that you lose height gradually. Otherwise your landing approach will either be very long or very steep.

Now reduce the throttle even further (or collective pitch). Concentrate on keeping the correct heading for the landing approach by carefully adjusting the tail rotor, but you should also be sure to keep the forward speed as steady as possible by keeping the nose inclined slightly down. This forward speed should not be too high, but you must avoid the machine stopping at all costs. At that moment the extra rotor blade airflow caused by the forward movement will cease, and rotor thrust will suddenly drop markedly. The model will tend to drop rapidly, and you will be forced to open the throttle abruptly (or raise collective pitch). The model will then become unstable, and the tail rotor will probably swing round. The helicopter is no longer coming towards you, but is now heading off in a different direction. This can be extremely confusing at first, and you will have no option but to open the throttle even more, fly off in the direction in which the model is heading, and try another landing approach.

Don't get worried about these comments before you start. Things are by no means as bad as they may sound, but it is vital for you to know what could happen *beforehand*, so that you are not surprised by your model's unexpected behaviour during landing approaches. Here is what you have to concentrate on: maintain approach heading with tail rotor, hold a steady forward speed with a nose-down

Fig. 128:
Advanced training: get hold of an inflatable paddling pool (about 2.5 m diameter), and fill with water. From as great a height as possible try to splash down in the dead centre of the water from a straight descent. If you rip open the tube with the tail rotor, you pay for the paddling pool . . . . .

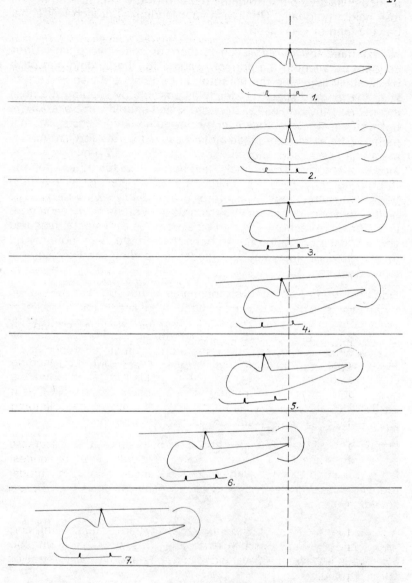

I

Fig. 129: I. Transition from stationary hovering flight to forward flight.

190

1. The helicopter is hovering over the take-off point in ground effect. The main rotor is trimmed so that the machine does not move in any direction with the cyclic stick at neutral. The tail rotor is trimmed to keep the model on a straight course (left stick).

2. To initiate forward flight, incline the main rotor forward (forward cyclic). The main rotor takes up a slight forward tilt.

3. With the stick held forward, the fuselage tilts forward. It stays above the take-off point for a moment longer.

4. As the fuselage tilts forward a little more, it begins to move forward. If slow forward speed is required, the main rotor should be neutralized now (cyclic stick back to neutral). If you want to speed up, keep the cyclic stick forward.

5. If the main rotor was neutralized at 4., forward acceleration will now slow down.

6. If the cyclic stick is left at neutral, the nose will rise slightly but will maintain a slight forward tilt.

7. The machine is now moving steadily forward, the fuselage still inclined slightly nose down. The main rotor is at normal setting. If speed rises too much, the main rotor is tilted back slightly (gentle back cyclic). Only a small command is needed here, so that the machine does not lose all its speed. If slow forward flight is required, no major change in rotor speed (throttle) is needed. Only when you require harder acceleration do you need to open the throttle to raise the rotor speed, to prevent the model losing height. If you want to climb out straight from take-off, open the throttle and raise the rotor speed. As speed builds up, the model begins to fly a gentle right turn. To maintain a straight course, apply gentle left tail rotor (left stick to the left).

---

attitude, and adjust the throttle/collective pitch to provide a descending approach, i.e. a steady rate of descent.

At this point the model can be allowed to come down to a landing just like a normal fixed wing aircraft, and just before touch-down the nose should be raised by pulling the stick back (back cyclic), as if applying up elevator. Be careful not to let the model start climbing again, which is likely if your forward speed is too high.

If your forward speed is just right, the model's sink rate will decrease as you raise the nose, and the forward speed will fall off. In an ideal landing, which is rare even with experienced pilots, the model touches down at the instant when the sink rate and the forward speed drop to zero.

A perfect landing approach is an extremely rare achievement, and the landing approach normally ends not with a landing, but with the machine in a stationary hover close to the ground; this is also true of full-size practice.

The model's landing approach, as described above, usually ends at a certain height in a stationary hover. In this situation we know from previous experience that hovering requires increased power. This means that you have to open the throttle again immediately before

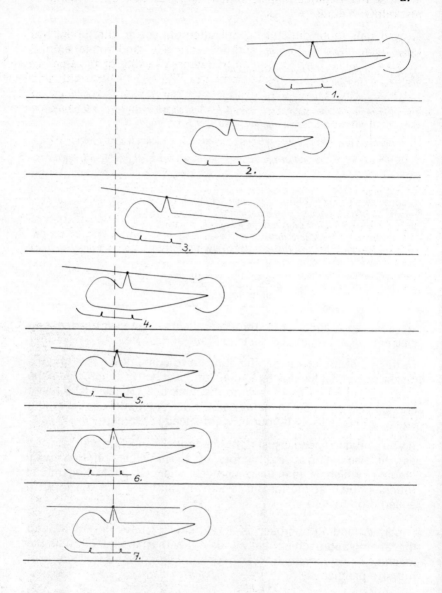

II

Fig. 130: II. This sequence of pictures shows how a helicopter is brought to a halt from slow forward flight close to the ground.

192

1. The model is flying slowly forward close to the ground. The main rotor is at neutral (cyclic stick). The fuselage is inclined slightly forward (as in 1/7).

2. The machine now has to be slowed down. To this end the main rotor is tilted backward (back cyclic). The helicopter slowly loses its forward tilt, and the fuselage returns to the horizontal.

3. The 'back' command to the main rotor is held on (cyclic stick back). The nose slowly rises, and a reduction in flying speed is noticed.

4. As the speed slowly drops, the rearward tilt of the main rotor is reduced (cyclic stick not so far back).

5. The model has now almost stopped. The cyclic stick can now be neutralized.

6. The model is now completely motionless. However, the fuselage is still inclined slightly back, and the model now has a tendency to start flying backwards. The main rotor system therefore has to be pushed slightly forward briefly (cyclic stick forward).

7. This short correction brings the fuselage horizontal, and if the main rotor trims are set correctly, the model will remain at the desired position with the controls at neutral. This will only last for a short time, however, and the model will soon try to head off again. You have constantly to apply small corrections to keep it in one place.

In the phases described, the main rotor speed (throttle speed) remains constant. It is only necessary to correct height above ground when the model's speed is higher. This is achieved by altering the throttle setting slightly.

---

the model comes to a halt, and control the model as in the previous hover practice sessions. It is a very good idea always to aim to land at a point in front of you where you are familiar with hovering. Now you can appreciate how important your hover practice was, and you will be very relieved if you find that you did practise enough.

If your landing approach goes wrong—and you can expect this to happen at first—on no account let the model crash-land out of sheer panic; it is much better to open the throttle again (or increase collective pitch) and carry out another circuit. Do 1 or 2 complete circuits to gather your wits (provided you know how much fuel is left in the tank), and make another landing approach.

Practise these landing approaches over and over again, although not to the extent that you neglect your hover practice. Once you have got the hang of flying circuits, you will find that this type of flying is much easier than hovering. It is tempting from then on to apply full throttle as soon as you start the motor, and carry out high-speed circuits followed by poor landings. There are many helicopter pilots who are able to perform marvellous high-speed aerobatics and can perform impressive high-speed 'beat-ups' along the strip, but who are not capable of carrying out a decent landing and a well-controlled hover. Please bear in mind at all times that practising the hover before flying off will show up any faults, and they are quite

RCHM–G

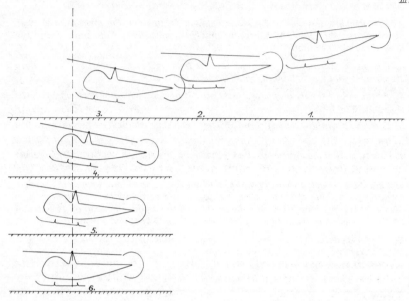

III

Fig. 131: III. This sequence shows a landing approach from a greater height. The approach is made in a basically similar way to that used for a fixed wing model. The motor is throttled back to a large extent. A reasonable forward speed is maintained by inclining the machine forward. The approach angle is steeper than with a fixed wing aircraft, and should be arranged so that you think the model will land 20 or 30 metres earlier than you want. In the flaring process described here, the approach angle is flattened out. In doing so, the machine takes longer to come to a halt (rather like a fixed wing model's ground roll).

1. The machine is approaching at relatively high speed, with a marked forward inclination of the fuselage. The motor is throttled back (left stick around neutral).

2. At a height of about 2 m the model is brought back to horizontal. This is achieved by applying back cyclic (rotor tilted back). The machine now flares out automatically— the throttle is still set low and passes into flat forward flight.

3. The cyclic stick is held back, and the model's nose rises strongly. This reduces forward speed more and more. By varying the backward inclination of the main rotor (cyclic stick back) the machine's altitude can be controlled. If you pull back too much, not only will the nose rise, but the model will gain height (in spite of the closed throttle).

4. Main rotor still tilted back; the model slows down further. The throttle is still closed.

5. Just before the model comes to a halt, the 'back cyclic' command is reduced, so that the model comes back to the horizontal. To prevent the model dropping out of the sky, the throttle has to be opened slowly to raise the main rotor speed. Torque will increase, of course, and the model will tend to rotate to the left. The more suddenly you open the throttle, the more marked will be this tendency. Moving the left stick

194

to the right will counter this tendency. This correction is only needed when you open the throttle, assuming that the tail rotor is correctly trimmed for hovering flight.

6. The model is now horizontal again, and motionless over the landing spot. Motor speed is now increased to the point where the model hovers at a steady height (left stick back). The tail rotor is neutralized again (left stick central). You now have the familiar stationary hovering situation. By slowly reducing motor speed the model may be set down vertically.

---

harmless at hovering altitude. If the motor is set too lean, for example, this will be most obvious in hovering flight, as the greatest power is needed in this phase. It is a great deal more unpleasant to carry out circuits with a badly adjusted motor, and then to find out when hovering prior to landing that the motor is going sour on you just when you need extra power to flare out.

Study Figs. 129, 130 and 131 to see what these transitions look like.

8. Aerobatics

When you have mastered hovering, landing, and all phases of flying circuits, there is one more area of flying for you to explore: aerobatics.

No matter what this term means to you, there are some things which need to be said before we start: there are some model flyers who scarcely learn to hover properly (I mean accurately) before they are dreaming of loops and rolls etc. There is nothing wrong with dreaming, but helicopter aerobatics demands in the first place absolute mastery of hovering flight. You should have this off to a fine art: fly a square circuit at constant height, no wobbling, straight legs, accurate corners etc.—go out and try that.

Now try precise rotation about the vertical axis. Constant height, constant rate of turn, ending precisely after 360°, etc.

How about hovering in a circle about yourself? Forwards, backwards, constant speed and height, no wobbling.

Take a camping table with you and try landing on it. Not just 'touch and go'—a proper landing.

Then there is transporting a load. Make a 'Schlüter pylon', place it on the ground, lift it up on one skid, fly round for a while, then set the pylon down again. At first just anywhere, then later on a definite spot. Or even on the camping table.

All these are aerobatics in helicopter terms, even if your spectators do not think so. And I know all too well that feeling you get when

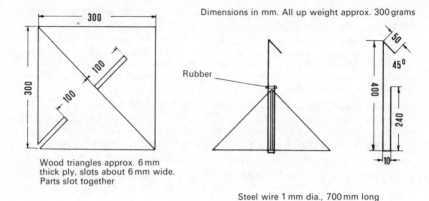

Dimensions in mm. All up weight approx. 300 grams

Rubber

45°

Wood triangles approx. 6 mm
thick ply, slots about 6 mm wide.
Parts slot together

Steel wire 1 mm dia., 700 mm long

Fig. 131a:
Dimensions and method of construction of the 'Schlüter pylon' for training and competitions.

a fellow modeller watches you carry out a superb hovering flight, claps you on the shoulder, and offers his condolences on the difficulty of making it fly higher . . . or the oft repeated questions: 'How high will it fly then? Can it fly really fast?'

That is when you forget yourself, push the helicopter into forward flight, pull up high, come round, fast low pass, towering stall turn, loop, roll, reversal . . . and you and your spectators will be satisfied.

Aerobatics with a helicopter? And why not? Aerobatics are a normal part of a fixed wing aircraft's repertoire, although a loop serves no purpose; it just looks interesting, is sometimes nice and round, and gives the pilot a chance to show off his skill.

9. Auto-rotation

The most important 'aerobatic manoeuvre' is, in my opinion, auto-rotation, as it can save the model if the motor fails. The model must be fitted with a freewheel, which releases the main rotor when the motor stops, allowing the rotor to continue rotating without the mechanics acting as a brake. The best way to practise AR is to fit a fifth servo for the throttle, so that collective pitch and throttle can be controlled independently. The model must, of course, be equipped with collective pitch control. Best results can be obtained with an AR switch on the transmitter (see page 102) and a motor set to idle rather than cut when the switch is used. Probably starting practice at half throttle is advisable, and you should learn the positions of the

196

transmitter stick corresponding to −20° to +2° rotor pitch, so that you know if you are flying with negative or positive pitch. See explanation later.

To start, fly a circuit at moderate speed at about 20 m height and when head to wind at 20−25 m from the intended landing spot, set pitch to 2° to 4° negative. Leave the throttle. Descend in a gentle incline (45°−60°) just as for a normal landing, correcting forward speed with the swashplate and rate of descent by pitch adjustment. At about 5 m (obviously higher than normal) raise the nose and halt travel with pitch. Reduce pitch to about −4° or −5°. If the model is stationary with steady pitch, nose down, fly off and repeat approach. Practise this approach until you can handle the sink rate smoothly and stop it at lower height.

Now to the serious bit. Switch the motor to its low AR setting and check any turn with the tail rotor. Follow the same landing approach, with negative pitch, and stop it (flare out) as before, using pitch control only; a skid height of 20−30 cm when stationary would be ideal. Now switch AR to full throttle, change to positive pitch (if separately controlled) and climb away straight ahead. You will be surprised at how much the model has in reserve to climb away steeply and smoothly, especially if the pitch can be set to 10°−12° positive.

With AR you must convince yourself that when the model flares out close to the ground there is always power to spare, though confidence in this requires working at. The tail rotor can virtually be forgotten − flight direction is controlled by the swashplate and the tail will weathercock.

There is an important point to remember. This loosely-described 'landing procedure' is not really true auto-rotation. Properly, an autorotating model will have a *positive* pitch of about 2° and a much flatter and smoother glide. However, it must be able to stop precisely and with the corresponding forward flight tilt, or the blades will cease to rotate, at which point it is too late for anything to be done. It would be flying to the limit of technical ability with no reserve for any mistakes or corrections and no reserve to flare out.

As a result, contrary to previous statements, a model helicopter in AR must be flown at a steep angle of descent with negative pitch, which then provides the energy reserve necessary to correct the flight path and gives more scope and rotor r.p.m. for flaring out. It is always a pleasure to watch an ace pilot cut his engine at 20−25 m, steer straight for the landing patch and plop it down gently right in the middle. Very enviable, but don't despair: the average pilot is happy if he can land halfway smoothly and somewhere near the landing spot. Especially if his motor has suddenly and unexpectedly cut out!

10. Aerobatics from normal flight

Normally a helicopter is trimmed out for stationary hovering flight, but such a trim does not hold good for forward flight. 'Normal' flight then requires forward stick for forward flight. However, for aerobatics it is better to trim the model for forward flight.

Generally speaking, this will require correction to the tail rotor, to prevent the model skidding, correction to lateral cyclic to ensure straight flight, and forward cyclic to maintain steady forward flight.

An important point: The main rotor should be turning as fast as possible at a low pitch setting. Apply only enough pitch to keep the model at a constant height in fast forward flight.

So: high speed, high rotor speed, low pitch.

It is also helpful if a trim switch as described in Section IV/7/E is available.

Upright loop: With the model trimmed as described, fly into wind and pull the nose up strongly, but not with a jerk. Correct lateral position, and adjust tail rotor if necessary (this is difficult).
Important: use initial momentum to carry the model to the inverted position, then you will have an excess of speed for the second half. If you judge it correctly, a second loop can follow the first. Do not alter pitch!

Immelmann: Start as for a loop. After half a loop, apply full lateral cyclic until the model is upright again. Correct attitude. Do not alter pitch.

Reversal: Straight approach, at a safe height. Apply lateral cyclic until the model is inverted. Then apply back cyclic strongly, but not with a jerk. After half a loop, pull out with the model in level flight. Do not alter pitch!

Inverted loop: Approach as for reversal, but from inverted perform a complete loop until the model is back where it started. Half roll out to upright. This manoeuvre only succeeds if the model is very fast, and does not lose too much speed in the half rolls. Once again: do not alter pitch!

Many combinations can be made from these basic manoeuvres. The basic rules are: keep your speed up, enter manoeuvres smoothly to

Fig. 131b: Inverted flight with a mass-produced Schlüter Bell 222 trainer helicopter.

avoid breaking the rotor. Always maintain the lowest pitch setting possible.

11. Aerobatics from inverted flight

The main problem is that certain functions are reversed in inverted flight. Left tail rotor is now right, and vice versa. Forward cyclic is now backward. Collective pitch is also reversed: up is now down. There have been attempts to master these reversed controls, but it really does seem virtually impossible.

However, all is surprisingly simple if the controls can be reversed from the transmitter. With modern transmitters, in which the servo direction can be altered by reversing plugs, this is fairly straightforward.

One three-way switch: reverses the tail rotor, while maintaining a constant setting; reverses longitudinal swashplate movement while maintaining a constant setting; reverses collective pitch from about −4° to +4°, and also reverses control movements (see IV/7/E/i).

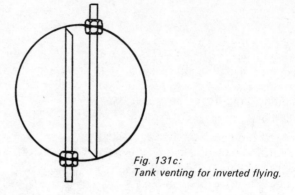

Fig. 131c:
Tank venting for inverted flying.

The motor must be kept at constant speed, and this is best achieved via a 5th servo operated by a separate function. Full throttle is then used all the time, and, as in all aerobatic manoeuvres, maximum rotor speed and minimum pitch angle is used.

Trimmed in this way, a model helicopter can carry out all the 'normal' aerobatic manoeuvres inverted.

Always assuming that the pilot has the skill . . .

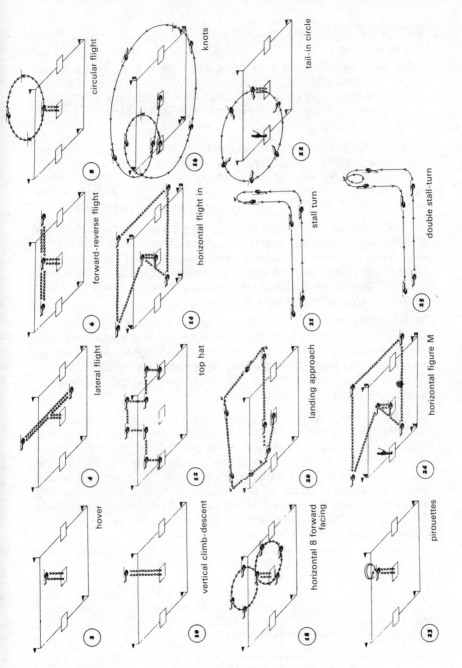

Fig. 131d: Basic aerobatic manoeuvres, mostly simple, to practise.

Schlüter Helicopter Cup

The Schlüter Helicopter Cup has been competed for over a number of years and was instigated to encourage beginners to try their hands at simple, straightforward competition. It has always attracted spectator interest, but while much can be learned from watching a competition in progress, nothing quite equals pitting one's own skills against others by actually taking part.

Very little space or equipment are needed to try your hand at the tasks set at your own flying site. Three 10 m squares need to be marked out as in the diagram below, one with two poles or pylons 4 m high set 6 m apart, as shown on the right, one with a table (centre) and one with a tower or stand about 2 m high. The programme is as follows:

1. Start with the two pylons and fly figure 8's round them. Height is not critical but the model must be low enough for it to be clearly flying round and between the pylons. Timing starts when the model first crosses the imaginary line between pylons (which must be within three minutes of being called) and the score is the number of 8's flown round the pylons in two minutes.

2. A bottle is stood on the table (centre square) and the model flies directly to it from the last figure 8 and knocks the bottle over. The model then flies between the pylons (right hand square) and returns to knock over the bottle again: an official replaces the bottle each time. Score is the number of knock-overs in two minutes, starting from the end of the first two minutes.

3. A pylon with a wire loop is placed on the tower (left-hand square) and the model must pick it up and deposit it outside the square. The method of pick-up and release is at the competitors' discretion. Each time a pylon is picked up an official places another ready for the helicopter to return and pick up again, so naturally a number of pylons must be available. Score is the number of pylons picked up and dropped outside the square in two minutes, running consecutively from the end of the previous task, i.e. each competitor has a total flight of six minutes with two minutes on each task.

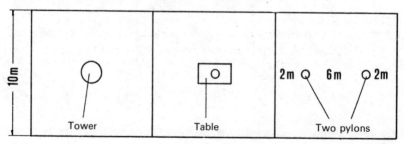

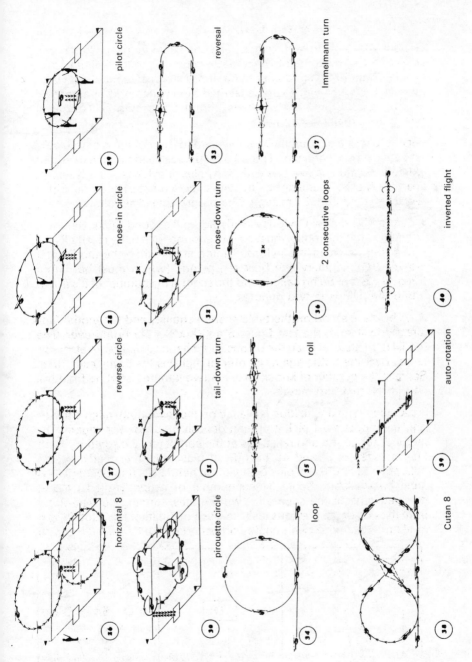

Fig. 131e: More advanced competition aerobatics.

203

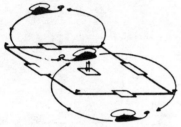

1. Hovering M   K=6

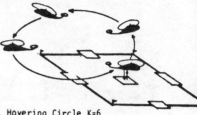

2. Hovering Circle   K=6

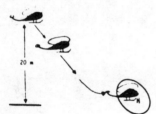

3. Horizontal Eight   K=8

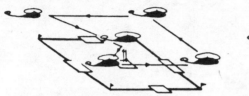

or

At Choice:
18. Autorotative Descent and Landing
                              K=9

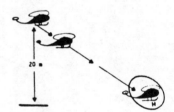

19. Landing   K=6

B. OPTIONAL MANOEUVRES

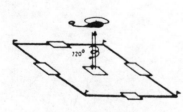

4. Double Pirouette   K=8

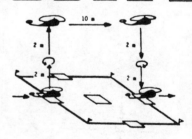

5. Top Hat   K=8

Fig. 131f (1—16): F.A.I. requirements for the first World Championships, held in Canada in 1985.

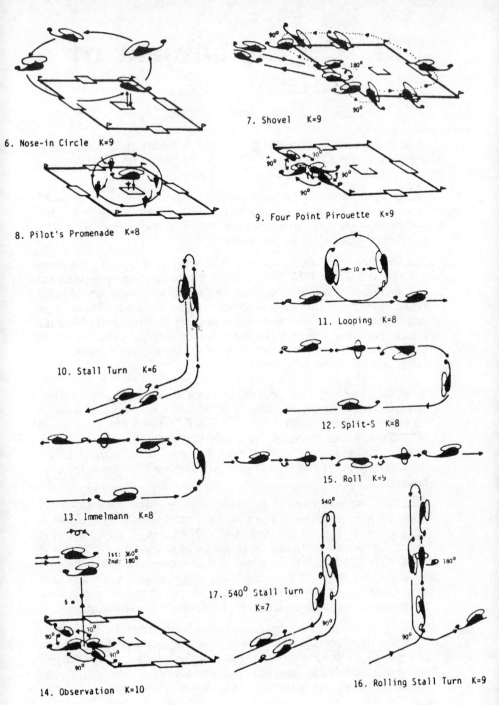

6. Nose-in Circle K=9

7. Shovel K=9

8. Pilot's Promenade K=8

9. Four Point Pirouette K=9

10. Stall Turn K=6

11. Looping K=8

12. Split-S K=8

13. Immelmann K=8

15. Roll K=9

14. Observation K=10

1st: 360°
2nd: 180°

17. 540° Stall Turn
K=7

540°

180°

90°

16. Rolling Stall Turn K=9

205

VIII. On the subject of safety

In all the enthusiasm for this fascinating flying machine, you cannot afford to neglect the subject of safety. Safety for you as pilot, and safety for onlookers and your flying colleagues.

A helicopter looks quite harmless and safe, especially when being flown by a skilled pilot. It stays in one spot, moves gently to and fro, and in any case you can easily jump out of the way. Right then, let's get right up close, it's so interesting . . . . .

The spinning rotor blades operate at fairly high revolutions. Between 1,000 and 2,000 R.P.M. That is 16 to 33 revolutions every second! In the case of a two-bladed rotor, this means that there are 32 to 66 chances every second for you to be hit by a rotor blade. The very tip would hit you first. This blade tip is moving at about 350—400 km./hour, according to rotor diameter and rotational speed. Quite a speed. By all means, mention these figures to curious spectators, but bear them in mind yourself too.

Now, this does not mean that the helicopter is an inherently dangerous machine. Flown sensibly, it is certainly not. For instance, a 10 inch propeller operating at 12,000 R.P.M. has a blade tip speed of 565 km./hr., and nobody pretends that model-flying should be labelled dangerous because of that. But you must be careful, and nobody enjoys getting his fingers in the way of a spinning propeller . . . . .

Exactly the same applies to the helicopter. Here too the watchword is—keep your distance, do not fly over spectators or 'buzz' them. Take off and land on the strip only. Of course, if you are skilful enough, you can start your motor away from the take-off area and hover over to it, but only if the model is correctly set up. It is absolute lunacy to try to fly the model over to the strip if you have just assembled it, and have not trimmed it out yet. In this case you *carry* the model to the take-off area, and that applies to experts as well.

Bear in mind that a helicopter not only flies forwards, but in any direction. The fuselage heading has nothing to do with the direction of flight. It can be extremely difficult to judge which way a helicopter will move and this is especially true of onlookers. A helicopter can 'wander off' in any direction. You will often see inquisitive folk standing close by the pilot under the assumption that they are behind the model, and that nothing will happen if they stay by the pilot.

Chase them away!

The model may suddenly be driven back towards you, perhaps by a gust of wind. You apply opposite control, but just to be sure, you walk a few paces to one side. If you do not fall straight over your spectators, you can be sure that they are still standing there, fascinated by your model, exactly on the spot which you have just left 'to be on the safe side' . . . . .

If it has not happened before, you will see all the people standing behind you as you attempt your first circuit, and you slowly turn round, following the model. These innocent folk are excitedly watching your model, and you now have to hold your transmitter aerial high over all their heads . . . . . so, make room for yourself; that constitutes a safety measure too.

Your starting assistant is an exception, of course. He stays behind you, walks to one side with you, turns with you, and occasionally reminds you that every fuel tank runs dry in the end.

That is another important point: a helicopter cannot be landed 'deadstick' like a fixed wing aircraft when the motor has cut. Auto-rotation does exist, of course, but usually if the motor stops suddenly, it is all too late. Your model will fall out of the sky. So keep track of your flying time, and come back part-way through the flight to check on the fuel level. In a sensibly designed model the fuel level can be seen at a glance.

Another safety factor which you should not neglect is the possibility of foreseeing future defects or failures. What I mean here is noticing sudden changes. For example, if you normally open the needle 3 to $3\frac{1}{2}$ turns to achieve a reliable motor run, and now suddenly it requires 4 turns or more, something is wrong! You can be absolutely certain that motor failure will occur in the near future. To carry on flying would be madness. Perhaps there is a speck of dirt at the needle, or maybe the feed pipe from the tank has split and is allowing air in; the fuel tubing may be kinked, or the tank loose, causing the fuel to foam, or perhaps the clunk weight is off in the tank, or the clunk filter is blocked; perhaps the carburettor has come loose, and air is being sucked in, or maybe this, or that, or something else. There are lots of other possibilities. Noticing the difference, looking for the fault and putting it right will save you a lot of trouble and expense.

Here is another example: you are hovering, when suddenly the model sounds different. Something is making a different noise. You may carry on flying and wait and see what happens; if you are lucky nothing will happen—the exhaust may be loose. But it is better—and safer—to look for a fault straightaway. The motor may have come loose, the gearbox may be out of oil, the tail rotor drive shaft bush may be loose, the cabin might have come loose, or maybe the undercarriage etc., etc., etc.

One more important example: the main rotor suddenly starts running roughly where it was always smooth; vibration increases and the controls feel different. This is an unambiguous indication of a defective pushrod, or a loose control arm, a loose blade fixing, a split rotor blade, or a blade whose root fixing has burst, or something similar. In this case safety has to be uppermost in your mind. You must not trifle with the enormous forces which act on the main rotor! When checking the model over, pay particular attention to the ball links. If the plastic part can be pushed onto the ball with virtually no resistance, it is time to replace it. The cost of a new link is out of all proportion to the danger of a worn-out one.

The same applies to replacement parts. It is very important that you use only the correct, original parts made by the manufacturer for replacements. If the designer has used heat-treated screws or locknuts in certain places, then he will not have done that because he has those items to throw away; they are a technical necessity.

And one more important point—a very important one! Before you switch your transmitter on, do make quite sure that your frequency is not in use. Every time! Also make it quite clear that you expect the same from your colleagues. No compromises here. This is for the safety of all of you.

If you bear all these matters in mind, then I only have one more thing to say:

'Have lots of fun, and good flying!'

IX. The most important calculations

The calculations quoted and explained in this section are not intended to help you to design a helicopter by mathematical means, so please do not look for instructions on how to use the calculations to build a helicopter. No such basic formula exists, since the factors which influence flight performance and behaviour are so many and varied that they could not possibly be reduced to a single formula, even if we use the latest technology available to us. Any attempt at squeezing all the basic values of a radio-controlled helicopter into one formula would be doomed to failure from the start. In any case, this approach would do nothing to help the average modeller understand the subject.

What interests us here are the basic principles and the units of measurement used in the helicopter world, and the variations when applied to model helicopters. These principles are by no means enough to base the design of a helicopter on, but they make it possible to compare designs with each other. Such comparisons are interesting when the results are compared with measurements made in actual test flights. You can then formulate and test your own theories, as well as drawing comparisons with subsequent models and your own experiments. This last possibility is important, as it is more than just interesting to compare any design or technical change which you make yourself with other models and their flying characteristics.

This sort of information and comparison is already well-known in the field of 'normal' fixed wing aircraft. For example, you can get an idea of the sort of performance to expect by checking the wing loading. The power:weight ratio also tells you quite a lot. In the same way, you know how certain wing sections will behave in different situations at various wing loadings.

It is just the same with helicopters. Here too there is a substantial amount of data that has been collected, and which can be summarized in certain formulae. These formulae make it possible for the experienced designer to predict the flying behaviour of his new model when he is drawing it up. All technical designs involve a mixture of positive and negative elements, and this is especially true of helicopters. The 'art' of the designer lies in playing down the negative aspects as far as possible, and in accentuating the positive aspects to the extent that they outweigh the negative aspects in the final analysis. A design which succeeds in this is itself a compromise in principle.

But now to the calculations. Let's start simply with:

1. Rotor disc area F (m.²)

This term means the area which is swept by the rotor blades in the course of one revolution. We are dealing here with virtually a circular disc, the outer diameter of which is the same as the rotor diameter. The rotor disc area can be calculated as follows:

$$F = \frac{D^2 \times \pi}{4}$$

Where D = rotor diameter in m., and π = 3.14

Example: Let us assume a rotor diameter of D = 1.2 m.

$$F = \frac{D^2 \times \pi}{4} = \frac{1.2^2 \times 3.14}{4} = \mathbf{1.13\,m^2}.$$

The rotor disc area forms a disc of slightly over 1 square metre total area.

2. Rotor disc loading R (Kp/m².)

This term means the ratio between the model's weight and the rotor disc area. It assumes that the model's weight has to be supported by the thrust produced by the rotor disc.

The rotor disc loading is calculated as follows:

$$R = \frac{G}{F}$$

Where G = model weight in Kp.
and F = rotor disc area in m².

Example: Model weight G = 4.5 Kp.
Rotor disc area (as in previous example) F = 1.13 m².

The rotor disc loading is calculated as follows:

$$R = \frac{G}{F} = \frac{4.5}{1.13} = \mathbf{3.98\ Kp./m^2}.$$

This means that each square metre of rotor disc area has to support 3.98 Kp. of model weight.

3. Area density C (%)

This term means the ratio of the surface area of all the rotor blades of a rotor system to the rotor disc area.

The area density is calculated as follows:

$$C = \frac{Z \times f1 \times 100}{F}$$

Where Z = number of rotor blades
       f1 = area of one rotor blade in m².
       F   = rotor disc area in m².

Example: Number of rotor blades Z = 2.
           Area of one rotor blade f1 = 0.033 m².
(This relates to a rotor blade 600 mm long and 55 mm chord).

Rotor disc area as calculated above F = 1.13 m².

The area density can now be calculated as follows:

$$C = \frac{Z \times f1 \times 100}{F} = \frac{2 \times 0.033 \times 100}{1.13} = \textbf{5.84 \%} \text{ of F}$$

This value in the calculated example means that the area of all the rotor blades amounts to 5.84% of the total rotor disc area.

4. Blade loading B (Kp./m².)

Blade loading means the ratio of the total model weight to the area of the rotor blades. The blade loading is calculated as follows:

$$B = \frac{G}{z \times f1}$$

Where G = model weight in Kp.
       z   = number of rotor blades.
       f1 = area of one blade in m².

Example: Model weight   G = 4.5 Kp.
            Number of rotor blades   z = 2
            Area of one rotor blade   f1 = 0.033 m².

The blade loading is calculated as follows:

$$B = \frac{G}{z \times f1} = \frac{4.5}{2 \times 0.033} = \textbf{68.18 Kp./m².}$$

This figure indicates that in our example 1 sq. m. of rotor blade area supports 68.18 Kp. This is, of course, only a theoretical, or comparative figure, as the area of the rotor blades is a great deal less than 1 sq.m. (0.033m² per blade). The blade loading is, however, significant in model helicopter terms, as it shows the loading of each blade, and how the blade's size (its lifting area) is related to the total weight.

For model applications you could simply calculate the ratio of the model's total weight to the number of rotor blades. In our example the model's weight is 4.5 Kp, and the number of rotor blades is 2, so each blade supports 2.25 Kp. However, this tells us nothing about the rotor blades' loading, i.e. the helicopter's 'wing loading'.

5. Peripheral speed V (m./sec.)

This term means the speed of a point rotating within the rotor system. The point will cover a greater distance or lesser distance in one revolution, depending on its distance from the rotor axis. The distance covered (in metres) in a certain time (seconds) also depends on the rotor's speed of rotation.

The peripheral speed is calculated as follows:

$$V = \frac{2 \times r \times \pi \times n}{60}$$

Where r = distance of point from rotational axis in m.
π = 3.14
n = rotor speed in R.P.M.

Example: Distance of point from axis r = 0.6 m (this corresponds to a rotor diameter of 1.2 m).
Rotor speed in R.P.M. n = 1500 R.P.M.

The speed of the blade tip can now be calculated as follows:

$$V = \frac{2 \times r \times \pi \times n}{60} = \frac{2 \times 0.6 \times 3.14 \times 1500}{60} = \mathbf{94.2} \, m/sec.$$

Multiplied by 3.6, this gives Km/hr. In our example 339.12 Km/hr.

The peripheral speed at the blade tip is—in still air—the same as the speed of the airflow at the blade tip. In the same way, the peripheral speed and airflow speed for any point on the rotor blade can be calculated. Only the distance of the point from the rotational axis (r) would vary.

6. Centrifugal force P (Kp)

Centrifugal force means the force acting radially outwards from the rotational axis, produced by the weight of the blades rotating about this axis. This force has to be withstood by the rotor blade fixings, feathering hinges etc. The centrifugal force can be calculated as follows:

$$P = \frac{G \times Vs^2}{9.81 \times r_s}$$

Where G = blade weight in Kp
           r_s = distance of blade's centre of gravity from rotational axis in m.
           Vs = peripheral speed of blade's centre of gravity in m/sec.

Example:1 Blade weight $G = 0.120$ Kp
          Distance of blade's centre of gravity
          from axis $r_s = 0.35$ m
          Rotor speed $n = 1500$ R.P.M.

The peripheral speed of the blade's centre of gravity Vs has to be calculated first.

$$Vs = \frac{2 \times r \times \pi \times n}{60} = \frac{2 \times 0.35 \times 3.14 \times 1500}{60} = \mathbf{54.95\,m/sec.}$$

With the aid of this figure, we can calculate the blade's centrifugal force as follows:

$$P = \frac{G \times Vs^2}{9.81 \times r_s} = \frac{0.12 \times 54.95^2}{9.81 \times 0.35} = \mathbf{105.53\,Kp} \text{ per blade}$$

Assuming the conditions as given (which are typical) the centrifugal force produced by each rotor blade, acting radially outwards from the rotational axis is 105.53 Kp per rotor blade!

(Finding the blade's centre of gravity is covered in Chapter IV/12, page 123).

Example 2:   Assume that as in Example 1 a rotor with calculated dia. of 1.4 m has an additional weight of 30 gm on the blade tips. Then calculate the following additional weight:

          Weight $G = 0.03$ Kp
          Distance from centre of gravity $rg = 0.7$ m
          Rotor speed $n = 1500$ R.P.M.
                                     (as in Example 1)

First again the peripheral speed of the additional weight:

$$Vg = \frac{2 \times rg \times \pi \times n}{60} = \frac{2 \times 0.7 \times 3.14 \times 1500}{60} -\textbf{109.9 m/sec}$$

From that calculate the flying power of the additional weight:

$$P = \frac{G \times Vg^2}{9.81 \times rg} = \frac{0.03 \times 109.9^2}{9.81 \times 0.7} = \textbf{52.77 Kp}$$

Solution:
As in Example 1, calculated mounting to the blade of the above-mentioned additional weight produces the following total flight power:

```
  Flight power of blade    = 105.53 Kp
+ Flight power of weight   =  52.77 Kp
  Total flight power       = 158.30 Kp
```

Example 3: With an aerobatic helicopter with special higher rotation speed and heavier blades the following values are produced:

Blade weight   G=0.180 Kp
Centre of gravity distance   rs=0.35 m
rotation   n=1900 r.p.m.

$$Vs = \frac{2 \times 0.35 \times 3.14 \times 1900}{60} = \textbf{69.6 m/sec}$$

$$P = \frac{0.18 \times 69.6^2}{98.81 \times 0.35} = \textbf{253.95 Kp per blade}$$

You can see from the examples that an increase of blade weight of 'only' 60 p from 120 p to 180 p (50%) and the increase of rotation of 400 R.P.M., from 1500 to 1900 R.P.M. (about 20%) produces an increase of flight power of about 148.42 Kp, from 105.53 to 253.95 Kp per blade. That is about 140% more power!

7. Power-weight ratio

This term is generally taken to mean the ratio of motor power, as fitted in the helicopter, to the flying weight. This power:weight ratio is usually calculated by the following formula:

$$L = \frac{N}{G} \text{ (BHP/Kp)}$$

Where N = Motor power in BHP
        G = Flying weight in Kp

This formula would indicate how much power is needed to lift one kilogram of model weight.

For model applications this formula is not very useful, as motor manufacturers usually only publish the absolute maximum power output of their motors, and this level of power is rarely achieved in practice. It can certainly not be considered as an effective continuous power level.

For this reason I think it is better to calculate the power:weight ratio for models on the basis of the ratio of motor capacity to flying weight. This formula also has its weak points, of course, as there are more and less powerful makes of motor in each capacity class. However, this is not all that important, as it is unlikely to be difficult to change from one make of motor to a more powerful unit in the same category, as mounting dimensions are generally similar. It is much more annoying, and usually impossible mechanically, to have to change from one size of motor to a larger class (or vice versa). For these reasons I suggest the following formula for calculating the power:weight ratio of model aircraft:

$$L = \frac{H}{G} \text{ (CC/Kp)}$$

Where H = capacity of the motor in cc
       G = model weight in Kp

Example: Motor capacity   H = 10 cc
         Model weight   G = 4.5 Kp

L is now calculated as follows:

$$L = \frac{H}{G} = \frac{10}{4.5} = \textbf{2.22 cc/Kg}$$

In this example, this means that to lift one Kp of model weight, a motor of 2.22 cc capacity has to be installed. This indicates, for example that a model weighing 5 Kp would require a motor of 11.1 cc. The answer here is a good 10 cc motor.

X. The development of the radio-controlled model helicopter

From my point of view the history of model helicopters is, in 1986, already 19 years old, since it was in 1967 that I started with the first practical experiments.

There is much that could be told: the nights of discussion with friends as to how a helicopter actually flies, what could be done with model materials, whether it was possible at all. Which motor? How heavy should the model be? What gear reduction? What type of gearbox? How best to make rotor blades, and how long, how wide and what section? A small rotor with narrow blades operating at high speed? Or glider wings rotating slowly around a shaft? Or this, or that, or the other? It was absolutely unknown territory. All we had was the desire to have a helicopter: it would be marvellous not to need a take-off strip any more, just to be able to hover, to lift up a weight and set it down again, etc., etc.

Where do such dreams come from?

For my part I had lost the urge to fly 'normal' model aircraft. Several times regional champion of Hesse in R/C 1, a few times in the top ten in the German National Championships—that was my absolute limit. I just did not have what it takes to be No. 1. Demonstration flights with low level inverted passes, balloon bursting and mock dog-fights had all become run-of-the-mill, and as (usually) every-thing worked out well, it was all becoming almost boring. So why not a helicopter?

And I was not the only one who thought this way. People were talking, machining and experimenting in many places, and the total number of hours sacrificed to the idea must be vast. Many gave up again, some kept going through to the first competition in 1968. A few kept on trying in spite of constant disappointments, had to put up with ridicule at their efforts, and spent their time in the workshop instead of with their families.

So my report can only cover part of the development, and only from my personal viewpoint.

My specific training? Precisely nothing! I was an engineer, to be sure, and a motor vehicles consultant, but how a helicopter flies? Not the least idea! I had to seek out information on the subject for myself, from specialized literature, visits to exhibitions, contact with the full-size machines. It was almost a second course of study for me, and a very intensive one at that. And of course there was a certain amount of ambition mixed in, as I wanted to master the subject.

My equipment? A medium-sized hobby workshop, a small lathe with drilling and milling attachments, a few metal-working tools, and 'normal' modelling tools. And this is where I started:

Fig. 132: My first helicopter (1967).

10 cc motor, 1.6 m rotor diameter, 4 function control, worm gear drive, 1 :10 reduction, BELL system of stabilisation and control, no collective pitch. Thrust control via throttle.

The model 'flew' many times in Autumn 1967, reaching about 50 cm altitude, and was surprisingly stable. It did not have a marked tendency to rotate, and would hover around for 10 or 15 m, without noticeably responding to the controls.

It was the result of more than six months' experiments aimed at finding the ideal blade size, gear reduction etc. There were just no points of reference. Bearing this in mind, this first result was extremely encouraging, and if the control throws were increased slightly, then surely it would . . . . . or so I thought!

Fig. 133: A simple 'clutch'

With the throttle set as low as possible, the main rotor was given a powerful *push*, and was engaged by pressing *downwards*. This worked quite well, but you could not disengage the clutch, and had to wait either until the fuel ran out, or the motor stopped —which usually happened quite quickly, as the cooling system was inadequate.

Fig. 134: Early 1968.

Number 2 was ready. Bell system again, but now with friction dampers and large control throws. And with collective pitch. The result: on lift-off, uncontrolled rotation around the vertical axis, constant difficulty with controlling the tail rotor, extremely vicious response to the main rotor controls. To sum it up—nothing worked. Tethering it did not help, nor did any amount of patience and pleading. It simply would not work. No comparison with the previous model. I started to broaden my knowledge by collecting technical books, and got advice from the 'full-size' experts. For the first time I found out about asymmetrical airflow, gyroscopic forces, flapping hinges, lead/lag hinges etc., and how complicated it all was. A big propeller just spinning round could not possibly work—so they said. And I followed their (well-meaning) advice.

Fig. 135: And then came number 3 in Summer 1968.

A semi-scale 'Sikorski S58' with all the frills: 5 main rotor blades, collective and cyclic pitch (directly-controlled), flapping hinges, lead/lag hinges with friction dampers, automatic switching to auto-rotation, freewheel, centrifugal clutch etc., etc. According to the literature on the subject, you needed all that for a helicopter! Sometimes it all worked, too, but . . . . . the pilot didn't have a chance! It would take off, and had a good climb performance, but what followed was a series of lightning-fast movements which were quite impossible to control properly. Nevertheless, I thought that I could master such a machine. A bit of practice, refine this or that . . . . . and generally wait and see what would appear at the first helicopter competition on 14/15 September 1968 at Harsewinkel. The attraction there was a few thousand DM for the best helicopter.

Opposite
Fig. 136: Harsewinkel 1968.

An obvious idea—and one often tried at that time: a drive system using two co-axial rotors. Here the normal propeller mounted directly on the motor constitutes the first, small rotor. The motor itself is mounted on the hub of the second large rotor, and drives it by torque reaction. The whole motor and tank, with balance weights, rotates. The system is amazingly simple, needs no gearbox, and transmits no torque to the fuselage. The tail rotor is also eliminated. Unfortunately, the effective thrust of the system is relatively small, as the efficiency of the small propeller is low. (Model by Ewald Dittrich)

Fig. 137: Harsewinkel 1968.

An attempt to improve the efficiency of the small propeller in a co-axial rotor system: the propeller sucks air in and pushes it into a sort of turbine, where the air is blown out radially to reinforce the drive system. The large rotor is meant to be driven not only by torque reaction, but also by the air being blown out by the 'fan'. The main rotor had five blades and was directly controlled. However, thrust was still too low for free flight. (Model by Christoph Hultsch)

Fig. 138: Harsewinkel 1968.

Another co-axial rotor system, in which the motor is suspended below the fuselage on the main rotor shaft. The motor is fed from two side tanks through the hollow main rotor shaft. The main rotor is fitted with a large stabiliser bar, which is controlled directly by a swashplate. The fuselage framework is made up from aluminium tubing. A tail rotor is also fitted for additional control about the vertical axis. This model also suffered from lack of thrust. (Model by D. Störig)

Fig. 139: Harsewinkel 1968.

A 'cargo helicopter' with co-axial drive by a suspended motor, rotating with the six-bladed main rotor. The main rotor was directly controlled and had no stabilising system. A tail rotor was also fitted. (Model by Schlatmann)

222

Fig. 140: Harsewinkel 1968.

A very interesting variant on the co-axial main rotor: two motors horizontally opposed, and connected via a reduction gearbox to the top rotor. Torque reaction rotates the two motors, complete with gearbox, fuel tank, and bottom rotor. Thrust control was by means of collective pitch variation. Direction of flight was controlled by tilting the whole rotor head. Fuselage heading was controlled by a movable fin, which was located in the rotor's downwash. (Model by Dr. Schlattman)

Fig. 141: Harsewinkel 1968.

A very competent, but extremely complex design, featuring a three-bladed rotor with collective and cyclic pitch, V-belt drive, centrifugal clutch, 100% metal chassis and tilting head control in all directions. Tail rotor control, and controllable tailplane. 10cc motor for power, 4.7Kg flying weight. (Model by Berkenkötter)

Fig. 142: Harsewinkel 1968.

A very interesting solution to the problem of adequate lubrication of the mechanical components: the model's reduction gearbox is fitted inside a large metal casing, into which the exhaust is led through a large pipe. The oil in the exhaust is deposited on the mechanical parts, and guarantees a constant level of lubrication. (Model by Knaf).

Fig. 143: Harsewinkel 1968.

The two-bladed main rotor of this model is directly controlled to provide collective pitch and also head-tilt control. The drive system involves a two-stage V belt system. An interesting feature: after the motor is started, it is swung to one side by a system of cranks. This places the first belt under tension, and the drive system is engaged. (Model by the Heinemann brothers)

Fig. 144: Harsewinkel 1968.

A very neat, beautifully made model of the 'Bell UH1D' made by F. W. Biesterfeld. The model was powered by a 10cc motor, and had a very carefully constructed, scale rotor head control system with collective and cyclic pitch. The main rotor blades were fully symmetrical, made of thin ply, and of hollow construction. The L.E. was fitted with 3mm steel wire to move the centre of gravity forward. The main rotor ran extremely smoothly, and the model exhibited a high degree of stability. The collective pitch system provided excellent control. Wilfried Biesterfeld was the only entrant in the competition to carry out a number of excellent hovering flights. These 'flights' only lasted a few seconds each, and the model never exceeded 50cm altitude, but caused much excitement due to the marvellous precision and stability. At this time it evidently proved impossible to achieve forward flight. Wilfried Biesterfeld gained second place in flying, and a very well-deserved first place in the static judging.

RCHM–H

Fig. 146: Harsewinkel 1968.

The jury took great trouble to judge the many designs, which were of widely varying concepts, reasonably fairly. Here I am trying to convince the judges that a radio-controlled helicopter can only fly with a rotor head fitted with flapping hinges, lead/lag hinges etc. At that time I was certainly convinced of this, and the judges had no choice but to listen attentively to my well-researched opinions.

Fig. 146 (opposite): Harsewinkel 1968.

With two 'flights' of about 4–5 seconds duration, and a height of about 3–4 m, I gained first place at this first helicopter competition (static judging 2nd place). Of course, you could not really call this 'flying' in the full sense of the word. It would be closer to the truth to call them the desperate attempts to avoid a crash immediately after take-off, by applying a few more or less correct control commands. The most I achieved in these 'hops' was to scare away the photographers who had come very close..... Nevertheless, the promoters—Simprop Electronic and Ikarus of Harsewinkel—fulfilled their end of the bargain and paid out cash prizes amounting to 9050 DM to the 12 active participants. The helicopter firm of Clever and Rietdorf also treated all the entrants to a total of 19 flying hours in a full-size helicopter—at a cost of 4750 Dm.

The outcome of Harsewinkel 1968 was the realization that a long and difficult path lay between us and proper control and flight of a radio-controlled model helicopter.

226

Fig. 147: I immersed myself even deeper in the problems, and made contact with Professor Just at the German Research Institute for air travel in Stuttgart. There the heart of the matter was tackled using a computer and simulator experiments. The following suggestions resulted: Three-bladed rotor, high rotor speed (1600 R.P.M.), large distance from the flapping hinges to the hub, heavy rotor blades. The 'Hughes 269H' was built on these lines. The rotor blades' inertia was increased by adding weights (not jets!) to the blade tips. The pull on the blades was now 150kg per blade! 10cc motor, radio-controlled belt tensioner to act as clutch. Collective and cyclic pitch. Several flights of 10–20 seconds duration, under partial control, at heights up to 20m. But take-offs were always desperate affairs, with many heavy, uncontrolled landings and frequent damage. The biggest problem: mastering the tail rotor! Experiments with gyroscope systems were unsatisfactory. Today I believe that this model could be flown with rotor speed control and the benefit of my present experience in flying.

227

Fig. 148: The problem of the apparently uncontrollable torque of a single rotor had to be overcome, and in Summer 1969 the 'FW 61' with its two contra-rotating rotors was completed. 10 cc motor, with power take-off at the rear to drive the two side rotors via a central distributor gearbox. Rotors with collective pitch for vertical and lateral control. Motor cooling by propeller. This was quite good. In calm conditions the machine would hover quite well at about 20 or 30 cm height. Lack of power and poor efficiency prevented it climbing higher. By inclining the nose down with the elevator, it was sometimes possible to achieve intimations of controlled forward flight.

Fig. 149: Autumn 1969.

The 'Twin rotor' idea would not go away. The mechanics were improved, and an impeller was used for good motor cooling. The very wide-based undercarriage prevented many an accident, and the new model certainly looked interesting. It also hovered quite well.

Fig. 150: The cooling impeller blew air out of the back of the fuselage in a powerful jet, and a controllable system of vanes in the tail was installed to direct the airflow up and down. This provided excellent pitch control. The fin was also in this airstream, and control of the rudder allowed rotation around the vertical axis. Here is one of the many 'test bench experiments'.

Fig. 151:
The drawback of the tail airstream: the model immediately set off forwards, and could not be stopped. A forcible stop made it rear up violently and it would fall onto its tail. The vanes were then replaced by a cover which could be swung in any direction. With the cover at 'neutral', the air exited radially and evenly. By tilting the cover, the airflow in one direction was emphasised, and a sort of control was possible. In very calm weather I was occasionally able to carry out controlled flights over about 20–30 m at a height of 30–50 cm: a partial success and very promising, but not the final answer.

Fig. 152: What had the others managed to do? I organised the first 'Helicopter meeting' at the helicopter base of Clever and Rietdorf in Saffig. There was much discussion and theorising, but nobody had managed genuine 'flight' yet. The best had been short, more or less uncontrolled hovering flights. But the germ of an idea had been sown: from this first event on I organised (and financed) a 'Helicopter meeting' every year. 1969, 1970, 1971 and 1972 at Saffig, and 1973 at Katzwinkel. Open to all, to all ideas, to all models. Four days long. Arrive Thursday, lunch together, flying. Theoretical instruction on Friday, lectures, discussions, test flights. Instructional films in the evening. Saturday: flying practice, attempts at improvement, a convivial evening. Sunday morning—the last joint venture, a quick drink—and travel home after lunch. Some participants came from England, Sweden, Belgium, Holland and Switzerland.

Fig. 153: At the last Schlüter 'Helicopter Meeting' held at Katzwinkel in 1973, there were over 80 participants registered for the theoretical instruction, and more than 30 flying models. The whole sports flying site was sealed off for the helicopter flyers, and there was intensive training in three groups. At the three take-off areas there were always several models in the air, and the workshop was a hive of activity. All makes of model were represented, there were friendly discussions, exchanges of information, and people helped each other mutually. An unpleasant aftertaste was left by a model manufacturer who flew in his demonstration team in the works aircraft in the middle of the event, and put on an advertising display: Idealism had to bow to commercial interests.

230

Fig. 154: Back to 1969.

The problems of the radio-controlled helicopter were not solved yet. On the contrary: everywhere the story was of stagnation, and the idea was spreading that model helicopters would never be a feasible proposition, and if at all, then only with almost infinite technical complexity. Was this really true? It almost seemed so. Nothing seemed to work. Bell control system, Lockheed stabilisation, gyroscopic aids, damped rotors, multi-rotor models, nothing. This made me furious: after all, had I not managed a few useful flights now and then? And I had learned a lot from my many experiments. I sat down, analysed all my earlier experiments, made up tables showing the positive and negative aspects, and made a point of avoiding reference to full-size practice in any way. I wanted a flying model, simple, robust, as little complexity as possible, and it should be able to fly and be controlled like a full-size helicopter. The theoretical result: single rotor, two blades, variable pitch tail rotor, no collective pitch control, rotor speed control via motor throttle instead, simplified 'Hiller' control system, using the aerodynamic damping and control assistance of the control paddles, a wide-based undercarriage, no extras at all. No sooner said than done: the old fuselage of the 'twin rotor' was cut down, fitted with the drive system, tail rotor and rotor shaft from the 'Hughes 269A', and the new machine was ready. It was Christmas 1969. It also had a new rotor head.

Fig. 155: This was the rotor head.

Fully articulated, two stabiliser bars (separate), 'Hiller' control paddles made of wood, with weights at the ends of the stabiliser bar, and cyclic control via the swashplate. Right on top can be seen the ballrace-mounted hook for flying tests in the tethered state. But this was only needed for a few minutes. I could tell immediately that this was the one. When I opened the throttle, the main and tail rotors speeded up at the same rate, and torque compensation was virtually automatic.

Opposite
Fig. 156: Maintaining heading was no longer a problem (I remembered my first ever helicopter attempt!). Advance the throttle, the machine lifts off, is stable, and—look— it responds to the controls. First 10 seconds, then a 20 second flight, then 30 seconds. Later it was over the minute. And that was in a strong wind, with heights up to about 10m, and in icy cold conditions. This was between Christmas and New Year 1969. Just one problem: when inclined forward fairly steeply, forward speed could not be braked, and the model slowly but surely would dive in. The only remedy was to land quickly. The reason was that the 'Hiller' control paddles developed powerful return forces, which the servos could not cope with. Then one day it hit very hard . . . . .

232

Fig. 157: This was the solution.

Fully universal rotor with a single, one-piece stabiliser bar fitted with metal paddles. The one-piece stabiliser bar resulted in the return forces of the two paddles cancelling each other out, so that the servo could control the paddles without difficulty. The remainder of the old mechanical system was fitted into a quickly assembled open model, and now it all worked. January/February 1970.

234

Opposite, top

Fig. 158: But the model had to look like something, and so I built the fuselage of the 'Bell Huey Cobra' around the mechanics. A centrifugal clutch was developed, an improved fan, an electric starter with V belt drive to the motor, a reduction drive tail-rotor gearbox, and a drive shaft running from the motor through to the tail rotor. The model flew — and how ! Now it was up to the pilot to get used to the controls. Next came the first real, exciting circuit — on 12th April 1970. Helicopter flying had become a reality. (See foreword and introduction)

Opposite, bottom:

Fig. 159: Whitsun 1970 at Harsewinkel, about eighteen months after the first helicopter competition: the first official demonstration of my 'Bell Huey Cobra' in the slow flight competition. I was terribly nervous, but I flew the model through the measured course, marked out with ropes to form a tunnel. It was obvious that I was really in control, and everyone was very excited. The only thing I had not attempted was backwards flight — and I lacked the courage and the experience.

Fig. 160: I continued practising circuits, and gradually improved my flying skill. I was constantly encouraged by the many cries of '. . . we want to see the helicopter . . .' and after an involuntary landing on a beer tent roof, I spontaneously announced a record attempt. Witnesses were drummed up, stop watches found, and then I flew the first World Record of 10 minutes and 36 seconds of uninterrupted flight. What does it matter that the record was not officially recognized because of incorrect procedure? (it was not notified) — I knew that it was successful, and thousands had seen it. What more could I ask for! And I was without doubt the first person in the world to do it.

Fig. 161: On 20th June 1970 I heeded all the regulations and set up an officially recognized world record time of 27 minutes and 51 seconds of uninterrupted duration, and distance in a closed circuit of 11.5 km. There were a few problems beforehand: It was so warm that the worm drive overheated. I fixed a 200 cc tank on the side of the fuselage, into which the gearbox oil was pumped, where it was cooled by the rotor's downwash. The fuel tank was enlarged to 1 litre, but I could only carry 0.8 litres to stay within the 5 kg weight limit. Otherwise I could have flown for longer; that was no problem. But I was quite satisfied as it was.

Opposite, top
Fig. 162: The reverberations from my success were fabulous. From all corners of the world came good wishes and invitations, and many people asked for information so that they could copy the model, or better yet, the finished mechanical components. Thus the first helicopter kits in the history of model flying were produced in late 1970/ early 1971—after a delay caused by a serious road accident. They were produced in my workshop, which rapidly changed into a mini-factory. Friends and the whole of the family helped; aluminium chips were everywhere, even in the bedroom, and the entrance hall was stacked full of polyester fuselages.

Opposite, bottom
Fig. 163: The gearbox was completely redesigned: It was now a spur gear/bevel gear arrangement, 1:3 reduction to the tail rotor, and 1:9 to the main rotor. The casing was a solid aluminium casting (hand made). Strong, reliable, and with excellent efficiency. Virtually all the parts were hand made. The whole kit cost 980 DM at the time, plus about 200 DM for the fuselage components, including the polyester fuselage. Orders came from all over the world, and my little hobby workshop was soon stretched to the limit. Besides, I still had my job as a motor vehicle consultant. I was looking for a partner.

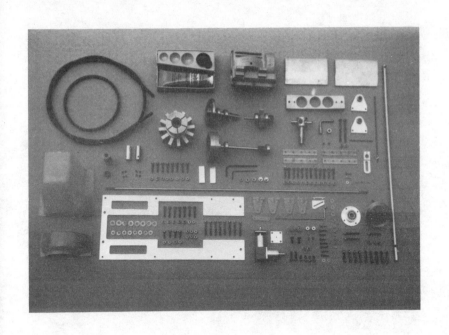

237

Opposite, top, Fig. 164: February 1972, Nürnberg toy fair.

The firm of Schuco-Hegi took over distrbution of the 'Bell Huey Cobra', and made the fuselage kit. The mechanics were made under my supervision in South Germany. The 'Bell Huey Cobra' opened up a new era in model flight all over the globe. The strong, solid design withstood many a hard landing—it had to, for nobody had any experience in helicopter flying. At that time everybody was starting from zero, and that is why I decided not to fit collective pitch control, to keep everything deliberately straightforward. This decision was vindicated in the long term.

Opposite, bottom, Fig. 165: The 'Bell Huey Cobra' conquers the world.

I received world-wide invitations to demonstrate the model, and was on the move all the time. I did not have enough time to accept all the invitations, but wherever I turned up, the enthusiasm was marvellous. Not that I was such an excellent pilot; but the fascination of seeing for the first time a helicopter which could obviously duplicate all the manoeuvres of the 'full-size' without difficulty, seized everybody. Enthusiastic clubs encouraged me to donate prizes, as here in Japan, where the winner of the first championships for radio-controlled helicopters receives 'Mr. Schlüter's trophy'. Almost every present-day expert learned to fly on the 'Bell Huey Cobra'.

Fig. 166: At the Nürnberg fair in February 1973, I presented my new 'D-S 22', which was to be distributed by Schuco-Hegi. This was a deliberately civil design, in contrast to the very military 'Bell Huey Cobra'. The 'D-S 22' had basically the same mechanics as the 'Huey Cobra', but now had a rotor head with flapping hinges, which improved flight stability. My original partner in manufacturing the mechanical parts decided to set up on his own at this time, and I had no choice but to take up kit manufacture myself. A host of sub-contractors made the parts for me, and I assembled them into complete 'D-S 22' kits. Thus I became a 'manufacturer'. The 'D-S 22' was the first to be offered on the market with floats, which not only made operation off the water possible, but also made practice on land much easier thanks to their large contact area.

Fig. 167: In 1972, F. W. Biesterfeld's design was taken over by the firm of Kavan, and they gave the one-time 'UH1D' a new suit of clothes: The 'Bell Jet Ranger'. At first the flying characteristics left something to be desired, as the rotor system, almost an exact copy of the Bell system, was not suitable for model use. In Autumn 1972 the decision was taken to adopt control paddles on the stabiliser bar, and from that moment on the model flew properly. As it had collective pitch control, the 'Jet Ranger' was an absolutely top class model in the hands of a capable pilot.

Fig. 168: At the Toy Fair in February 1973, Graupner showed their first helicopter: This was the 'Bell 212 Twin Jet', and was made by the motor manufacturers, Bernhardt. It featured a 10cc motor, collective and cyclic pitch, and a largely pre-assembled mechanical arrangement, which was installed in a polyester fuselage. The 'Hiller' system of control was adopted, with collective pitch control superimposed. The undoubted advantage was that thrust was more directly controllable, and when adjusted correctly, it was easier to fly. Nevertheless, it did not provide a solution to the protracted learning process which the beginner still faced, although this model looked very easy to fly when demonstrated by experts. Here is Manfred Kufner at Sywell, England, in Easter 1973.

240

Fig. 169: In late August 1973, Schuco-Hegi got into marketing and financial difficulties, and I was left with several thousand pre-fabricated helicopter components on my hands. New developments (the later 'Heli-Baby') were shelved, and my only course of action was to set up my own distribution network. The 'Gazelle' was produced, which had the mechanics of the 'D-S 22' plus collective pitch, and early in 1974 I had my own stand at the Nürnberg toy fair as an independent distribution company. 'Schlüter Modellbau' was born, and many friends said: 'You should have done that in 1970 . . !'

Fig. 170: At about the same time my former partner in the production of mechanical parts began production of the 'BO 105', which was distributed by Rowan and Klinger, using parts originally destined for me. This model was identical to the 'Bell Huey Cobra' and the 'D-S 22' apart from the new fuselage and a few small alterations. The model could be fitted out with many scale details, had cyclic pitch control, rotor speed thrust control, and flew very well.

241

Fig. 171: Early in 1975 the era of the 'minis' arrived. There was a general demand for a simple, fast building helicopter, and the problem of transport demanded a solution. The idea I had had in 1973, of an open-structure helicopter with self-supporting metal chassis, was resurrected, and the result was the 'Heli-Baby'. 6.5 cc motor, rotor diameter of 1 m, cyclic pitch control only (it was intended to be simple), and fully articulated main rotor. The model was enthusiastically received. The price was within many people's reach, and the ease of maintenance, robustness and stability—especially in hovering flight—made many friends. From 1976 the 'Super Heli-Baby' was also offered, with collective pitch control.

Fig. 172: At the same time Graupner produced their own mini-helicopter, the 'Bell 47G'. This model featured excellent detail design and innovative manufacturing techniques; great emphasis was placed on the use of injection-moulded plastic parts, and the model could be assembled unusually quickly. The kit even included the motor and fuel tank. Building a helicopter was no longer a technical problem. The one thing the modeller still had to do was to really tackle the subject of helicopter flying in a determined way; there has never been a way round this. It just is not possible to learn to fly a helicopter in a day—just as it is not possible with a 'normal' fixed wing model....

Opposite
Fig. 173: The first German Helicopter Championships were held at Braunfels in 1975, for those who were already skilled in the art. The 'top three' were:

1st: Michael Bosch with a 'Bell Jet Ranger'.
2nd: Dieter Schlüter with a 'Schlüter Gazelle'.
3rd: Heinz Elsässer with a 'Schlüter Gazelle'.

For those less adept, training stands appeared on the market. The model could be attached to a movable platform or a retainer, which allowed it to move in all directions within certain limits. This was an excellent way of gaining that initial experience without breaking anything. The picture shows the training stand that I produced, in which the model (Heli-Baby) is suspended at the centre of gravity by a yoke. This allows it to react to the controls almost as if in free flight. The model can also 'climb' about 20 cm.

243

Fig. 174: Early in 1976 another 'mini' helicopter appeared: Kavan's 'Alouette 2', with an open framework fuselage, a centre fuselage section of plastic, with a 6.5 cc motor, a large cabin, and cyclic main rotor pitch control, using the 'Hiller' system plus additionally controlled main rotor blades, without collective pitch.

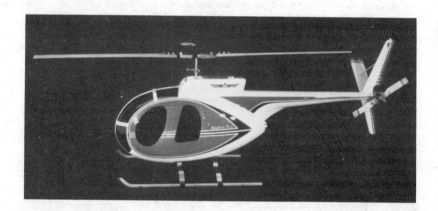

Fig. 175: The fuselage of the 'Hughes 500' helicopter is available to fit the 'Heli-Baby' and the 'Super-Baby' to please those who value appearance. This helicopter is well-known in the USA, and is often seen in Germany. The fuselage is simply fitted around the model, and has no load-bearing function. The photo shows the scale version, with the tail surfaces set well back. The model proved impossible to fly in this configuration. When forward flight was initiated, the rotor downwash was directed backwards, and struck the tail surfaces. The result was a powerful downward pitching movement of the tail, and the model would rear up strongly. For practical use, the tail surfaces were fitted lower down and further forward, where they are constantly in the rotor downwash.

Fig. 176: The 'state of the art' in early 1977: The 'Bell 222'. In this model I tried to incorporate all the knowledge and experience acquired up to that time: 10 cc motor, a strong, self-supporting metal chassis as in the 'Heli-Baby', a large cooling fan, bevel gear drive to the tail rotor, 10 mm diameter main rotor shaft, cyclic pitch control with control paddles, almost rigid rotor with high mast moment, a mixing lever integral with the rotor head for collective pitch control, collective pitch control independent of cyclic pitch control, torque compensation for the tail rotor, a large tail surface outside the main rotor downwash, a simple, solid design, good accessibility to all parts, 500 cc fuel tank at the centre of gravity, engine starting via electric starter from above or from side using a belt etc., etc. All this was clad in a moulded scale fuselage of the latest 'Bell 222', a cruising/commercial helicopter with 2 turbines. Large side hatches provide excellent access to the most important mechanical parts, for fuelling, needle adjustments, trim corrections etc.

Fig. 177: This is the special feature of the 'Bell 222': As it has a self-supporting metal chassis, the model can be flown with just a simple cabin and the rest completely open. This makes maintenance, adjustment and flying practice much easier, especially for the beginner. In this configuration the model can be attached to the training stand for practising. When the pilot has mastered the techniques, the fuselage moulding can be fitted very simply, and the skids can even be replaced by a tricycle undercarriage. Shown here is the 'Bell 222' in the open trainer version, fitted with an experimental tuned pipe exhaust.

245

Fig. 178:

No line of development is ever concluded, and when we consider the past years, it is really amazing just how much has been achieved in the history of the radio-controlled model helicopter. When I carried out my first flights in 1970 I was so enthusiastic that I was quite certain this was the beginning of a new era in model building—and I was correct. But I never even dreamed that progress would be so very rapid. The Bell 222 model, which quickly established a world-wide reputation, can reasonably be claimed to have ushered in the aerobatic phase of model helicopter development and has been a major factor in extending the popularity of model helicopter flying.

Fig. 179
The basic design philosophy of the Bell 222 proved so good that it became the basis of the 'System '80'. A variety of extension stages were developed to fit the proven cantilever chassis, and this made it possible to produce a large number of different models in a variety of versions at different price levels. Shown here is the Bell 222, consisting of a number of GRP mouldings, fitted with the aerobatic rotor. Loops, rolls, reversals, Immelmanns, present no difficulties. It is equally possible to fit a simple rotor, and have a lot of fun at lower cost.

Opposite, Fig. 180:
Early in 1979, Graupner produced a model which also carried the name Bell 222. This was basically the mechanics of the '212 Bell Twin Jet' of 1973, which had been converted to a cantilever structure by the addition of a set of metal plates. The new rotor head had no stabiliser bar, and the main rotor blades were directly controlled. The mechanics could be fitted with a vacuum formed fuselage, or a Bell 222 fuselage in epoxy resin.

247

Fig. 182
Since 1980, the System '80 has included a GRP body of the 'Jet Ranger II'. This popular helicopter, which is particularly well known in the USA, impresses all who see it, and the BELL design team's fuselage shape has a timeless elegance. The advantage of this model is that it can be fitted with any of several rotor heads to suit your pocket and your needs.

The 'BO 105' shown here rapidly achieved popularity, and was designed as part of the System '80. It can be fitted with a simple rotor head without collective pitch, the well known two-bladed aerobatic rotor, or the newly developed four-bladed rotor. The four-bladed rotor is unusually stable, is directly controlled without recourse to a stabiliser bar, and features flapping and lead/lag hinges.

Fig. 183
The original Schlüter Bell 222 gained world-wide popularity, and more have been built than any other model. This was especially true in the USA, where it received tremendous acclaim under the name of the 'Heli-Boy'. In 1978, for example, the Schlüter 'Heli-Boy' represented over 80% of entries at all competitions, and won all the first places bar one, including the US national championships. By 1979 'ordinary' aerobatics with the Schlüter 'Heli-Boy' were no longer enough. Auto-rotation was an everyday event, and was included in every contest schedule. In mid-1979, the US champion Mike Mass successfully carried out prolonged inverted flight with a standard kit Schlüter Heli-Boy, with only minor modifications—as if it were nothing special at all.

Fig. 184
The System '80 has been extended to include a simplified rotor head, which was basically the S rotor of the DS 22 and Gazelle; a design with years of success to its credit. The modified rotor was intended to provide a better starting point from the point of view of price and simplicity. The higher performance of the System '80, together with light control paddles, make this model very manoeuvrable and lively, and even experienced pilots find it a great pleasure to fly. The complete kit with cabin, rotor, blades and all accessories is offered in Europe under the name of 'Heli-Boy'.

Fig. 186: The SX 81 is essentially the same mechanically as the 'Cheyenne' but is fitted with a simpler fuselage employing less complex mouldings. This non-scale appearance could offset the very good aerobatic properties for contest use, but for sport flying is not important — at any distance fine scale details are hardly visible.

*Opposite
Fig. 185:*

The latest production model from the Schlüter stable is the Cheyenne, a scale model of the US combat helicopter of that name. A new drive system was developed for this model to allow a much lower profile design. This brings the Centre of Gravity higher in relation to the rotor, so that rolling manoeuvres can be flown much more easily and over a greater distance. The model features an AR freewheel device and retracting undercarriage as standard, and it is unusually fast. The stub wings make the model more easily recognizable in flight, and also contribute to smoothness of flight and manoeuvrability. It can be flown with any of the rotor heads in the System '80.

251

Fig. 187: The 'Superior' resulted from the wish of many model fliers to have a robust and efficient 'long life' helicopter. Just about every bearing carries a ball-race – in the standard kit there are some 40 and it would be possible to incorporate nearly 50. One effect is much more precise control of pitch and blade position.

Fig. 189: The Schlüter 'Agusta 109A' is an extremely accurate reproduction of the full-size prototype built round the mechanics used in the 'Heli-Star', 'Superior' and 'Champion'. A true-scale three-blade rotor can be fitted.

Opposite
Fig. 188: The 'Heli-Star' is a further development of the already legendary Schlüter Bell 222 trainer. The head is more robust and has axial blade pinning, the tail rotor is bevel geared and all parts have been strengthened. This model will replace the Bell 222.

Fig. 191: The BK 117 with four-blade rotor, a very accurately detailed reproduction of the team of Bölkow and Kawasaki's work on flight equipment. The model can fly with a normal two-blade rotor or with quite realistic four blades. Rotor blades are film-covered wood without extra reinforcement or added weight and are direct-controlled without stabilisers. This takes a little getting used to, but once competent flight control is excellent and the flight appearance and rotor noise are very convincing.

Fig. 190: The Schlüter 'Champion' represents a new approach with very light all-metal construction, which suggests future development taking advantage of superior dimensional stability. Perhaps the outstanding feature, though, is the greater stability and easier control provided by the mounting of the stabiliser bar under the rotor head.

Fig. 192: A stylish and lightweight model with exceptional flight performance is the Bell 'Long Ranger' fitted with 'Champion' mechanics and a 'Champion' two-blade aerobatic rotor.

255